HOT AND COLD LANDS

Michael Shorthouse

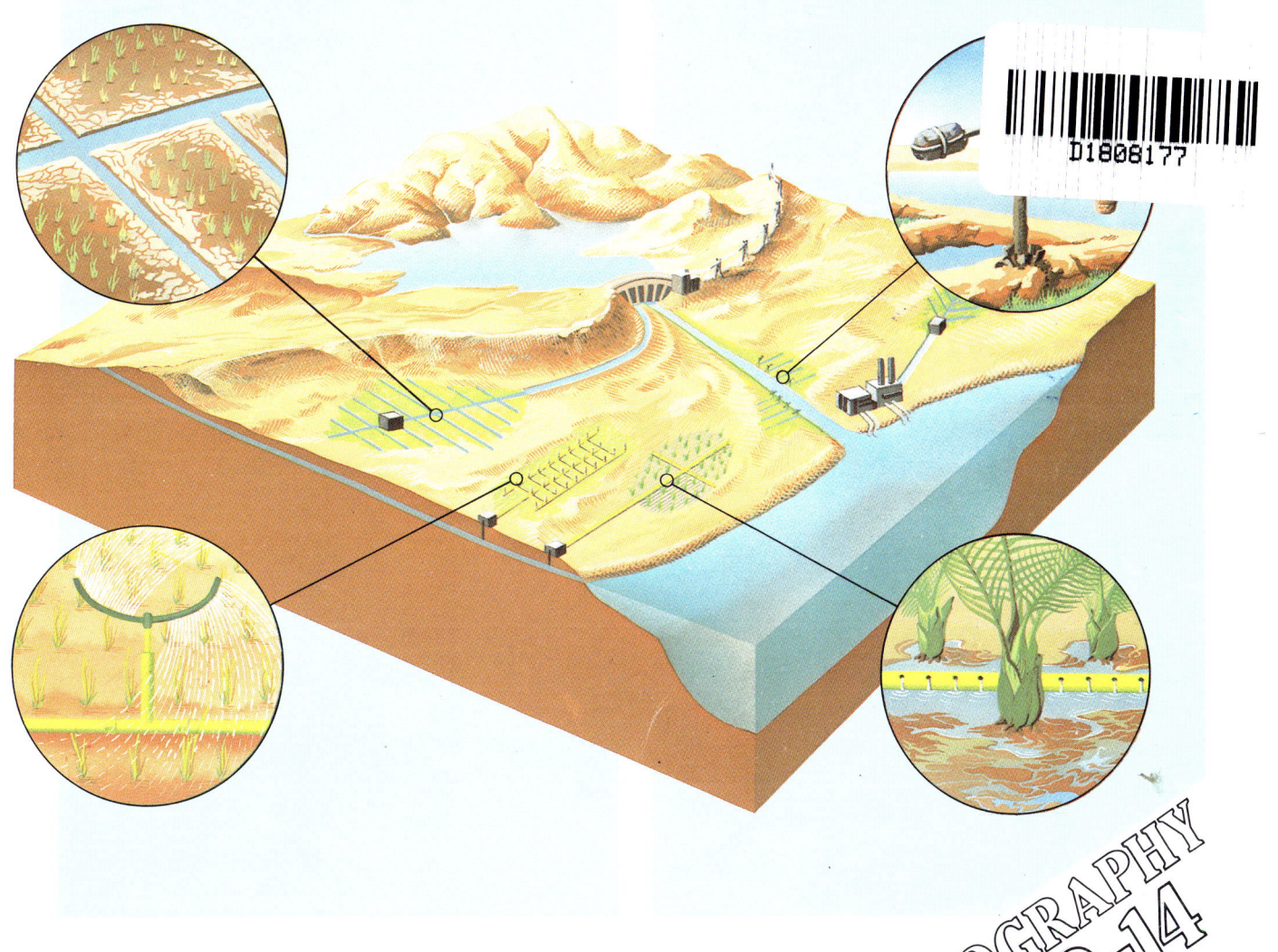

Macdonald

GEOGRAPHY 10-14

A MACDONALD BOOK

© Macdonald & Co (Publishers) Ltd 1984

First published in Great Britain in 1984 by Macdonald & Co (Publishers) Ltd London & Sydney

A member of BPCC plc

ISBN 0 356 09351 4

Printed and bound
by New Interlitho, Italy

Macdonald & Co (Publishers) Ltd
Maxwell House
74 Worship Street
London EC2A 2EN

Acknowledgements

The publisher would like to thank the following for permission to reproduce photographs:

(Numbers refer to pages and T, B, C, L, R, indicate top, bottom, centre, left and right)
4 B Spectrum Colour Library, T ZEFA; 5 T ZEFA, B Peter Boothroyd; 6 Spectrum Colour Library; 9 G.R. Roberts; 10 Scott Polar Research Institute, Cambridge; 12, 13 R Michael Shorthouse, 13 R J. Allan Cash Photolibrary; 14 T National Film Board of Canada, courtesy Canada House; 15 Courtesy of the Trustees of the British Museum; 17, 20 ZEFA; 22 T, BL Swiss National Tourist Office, BR ZEFA; 23 B Swiss National Tourist Office; 24 T Spectrum Colour Library, B ZEFA; 25 Spectrum Colour Library; 26 FAO; 28 T Tony Morrison, TC ZEFA, BC Michael Shorthouse, B Barnaby's Picture Library; 29 ZEFA; 30 Popperfoto; 31 Barnaby's Picture Library; 32, 33T Alan Hutchinson; 33 Colorific/P. Tweedie; 34 Christian Aid; 36 M. Sparrow/MEPhA; 39 CWDE/Kaiser Industries; 40 Tony Morrison; 42 T, B Alan Hutchinson; 44 T ZEFA, B Alan Hutchinson; 46 Marion Morrison; 47 Alan Hutchinson

The publisher would like to thank Dr Arno Peters and Universum-Verlag, Munchen-Solln, for permission to use the 'Peters projection' for all maps of the world depicted in this book.

Cover photograph:
Road construction near Zilfi, Saudi Arabia (Topham)

The illustrations are by Robert and Rhoda Burns/ Drawing Attention, pp. 9, 11, 12, 15, 17, 22, 35, 38, 45; Gary Hincks, pp. 21, 37, 41, 43; Kevin Maddison, pp. 16, 19, 20, 30, 31; Raymond Turvey, pp. 7, 8, 9, 26, 27

Extracts from *The Fearful Void* by Geoffrey Moorhouse, Copyright © 1974 by Geoffrey Moorhouse, reprinted by permission of Hodder and Stoughton Limited.

GEOGRAPHY 10-14

Series Editor: Richard Kemp,
Head of Humanities Faculty,
Lord Williams's School, Thame

Hot and Cold Lands

Editor: Michèle Byam
Designer: Sally Boothroyd
Picture Research: Suzanne Williams
Production: Susan Mead

Series Consultants:
Barbara Hamnett, Head of Geography,
J.F.S. Comprehensive School, Camden
David Robinson, Headmaster, Blue Coat School, Dudley
Michael Storm, Staff Inspector of Geography, Inner London Education Authority
Michael Weller, Co-ordinator of PGCE Programme, Bulmershe College of Higher Education, Reading
David Wright, Lecturer in Education, University of East Anglia, Norwich

The author wishes to thank the Swiss Federal Statistics Bureau and British Petroleum for information provided for use in the text.

Contents

Hot and Cold Places

There are some places on Earth where it is very difficult for people to live. Like most plants and animals, people need sufficient warmth, water and nourishment in order to stay alive. Without them they cannot survive.

Calama, near Antofagasta in the Atacama Desert of South America, may well have received no rain for 400 years or more. It is probably the driest place in the world. Farmers would hardly choose to live there! Death Valley in California is well named. With summer temperatures reaching 45°C, it is hot enough to fry an egg on the rocks. Its highest recorded temperature is 56°C.

Figure 1: Hudson Bay Mountains, near Smithers, British Columbia

Water freezes when the temperature falls below 0°C. At about −25°C diesel oil freezes in engines that are running. At about −35°C if someone without gloves touched something metal their skin would stick to it instantly. Verkhoyansk in northern Siberia, U.S.S.R. has winter temperatures that fall to −65°C.

Many of the places in which it is very difficult to live are the last great wild places, or wilderness areas left on earth. Although life is difficult some people have settled in these lands. To survive they have adapted the ways they live.

Today the wilderness areas are still a challenge to people. They contain many of the **natural resources** that humans want. In this book you will see some of the ways in which these natural resources have been developed. These developments have brought changes to these extreme environments and the people already living in them.

Figure 2: The Pagsanjan River in the Philippines

1 The photographs on these pages (Figs. 1, 2, 3 and 4) show four different environments in hot and cold lands. For each photo explain briefly why you think it difficult for people to live there.

2 Read the extracts from the writings of Ernest Shackleton and Geoffrey Moorhouse. In your own words say what it was that made the environments they were living in so difficult.

3 Use your atlas to find the following places and mark them on your own copy of a world map.
(a) Antofagasta, Chile; Death Valley, U.S.A.; Verkhoyansk, U.S.S.R.
(b) The places shown in the photos.
(c) The areas being explored by Ernest Shackleton and Geoffrey Moorhouse.

4 In which of the four areas shown in the photos would you find it most difficult to live? In which would you find it easiest to live? Give reasons for your choices.

Figure 3: Tundra ponds on the Arctic coastal plain in Alaska

7th January, 1909. 'A blinding shrieking blizzard all day, with temperatures ranging from −50°C to −60°C of frost…'
8th January, 1909. 'I feel this march must be our limit. We are so short of food…it is hard to keep any warmth in our bodies between the scanty meals…'

(Ernest Shackleton (Sir), *Antarctica*, 1909.)

Figure 4: The El Oued oasis, Grand Erg Oriental desert, Algeria

'It was a beautifully clear morning when we set off, but by nine-thirty the sandstorm had blown up again. Visibility dropped to a quarter of a mile but we could not afford to stop as it was vital to find water as soon as possible. We had to keep going through this lacerating void of khaki and white.
'By four-thirty the storm had died again and slowly the sun reappeared, the visibility increased and we could see for several miles around. There was not a rock or a tree in sight − nothing but empty sand.'

(Geoffrey Moorhouse, *The Fearful Void,* 1974.)

Where are the Hot and Cold Lands?

This book looks at four types of environments where life is difficult. Where they are can be seen in Map A (Fig. 2).

Since early times people have depended on farming to stay alive. In many parts of the world this is still true. In the areas marked on Map A farming is usually difficult and sometimes impossible. In the deserts there is not enough regular rainfall. High up in mountains it is cold and the steep slopes have little soil. In the rainforests the trees have to be cleared from the land, and then the soils may be easily ruined. In the cold lands there is not enough warmth for crops to ripen. Because of these difficulties, few people choose to live in these places.

Map B (Fig. 3) shows the areas of the world that have only a few people living in them. They all have fewer than 3 inhabitants for each square kilometre of land.

A camel plough in Tunisia

1 Look at Map A and estimate what percentage of the Earth's land surface is made up of areas where it is difficult to live: 30%; 50%; 70%?

2 On your own copy of a world map carefully transfer the information from Map A. Colour deserts in yellow, cold lands in blue and rainforests in green. Remember to give your map a title and key.

3 The table in Fig. 1 lists the names of places with difficult environments:
(a) Copy out the table.
(b) In your atlas find each place and then mark it onto your copy of Map A. (You may need to use a key to keep your map neat.)
(c) On your table fill in the second column by deciding which type of difficult environment is found at each place.
(d) Locate each place on Map B. Complete the third column by saying whether it has more or less than 3 people per square kilometre.

4 Compare Maps A and B:
(a) What similarities are there between the information shown on the two maps?
(b) Explain in your own words why these similarities exist.

5 Select one of these places where life would be difficult and imagine that you had to live there. How do you think you could make life more pleasant for yourself? Give details and include illustrations to show what you would do.

Name of Area	Type of Difficult Environment	Pop. Density above or below 3 per km^2
1. Alaska (North America) 2. Alps (Europe) 3. Amazon Basin (South America) 4. Andes (South America) 5. Antarctica 6. Arabia (Asia) 7. Atacama (South America) 8. Congo Basin (Africa) 9. Greenland (North America) 10. Himalayas (Asia) 11. Kalahari (Africa) 12. New Guinea (Oceania) 13. Rockies (North America) 14. Sahara (Africa) 15. Siberia (Asia)		

Figure 1: Difficult environments

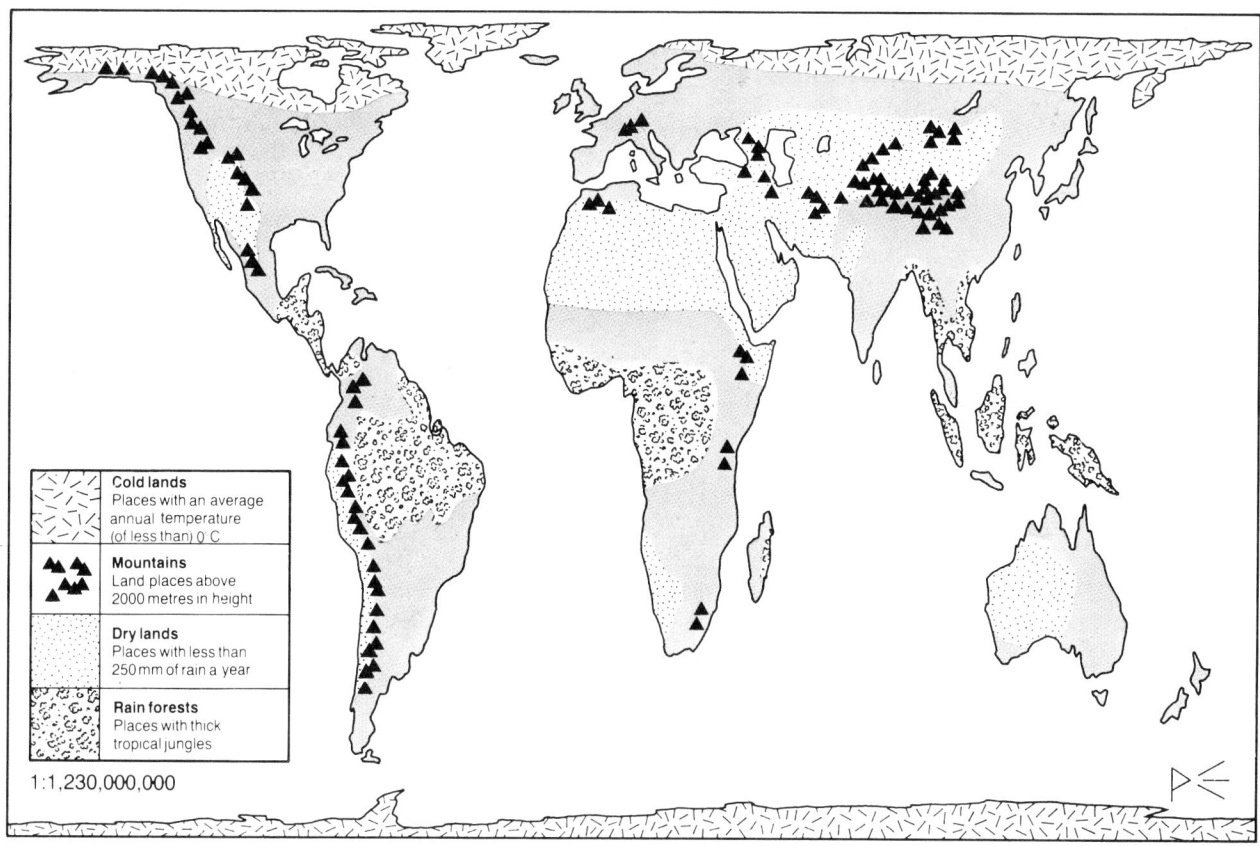

Figure 2: Map A

Cold lands
Places with an average annual temperature (of less than) 0°C

Mountains
Land places above 2000 metres in height

Dry lands
Places with less than 250 mm of rain a year

Rain forests
Places with thick tropical jungles

1:1,230,000,000

Figure 3: Map B

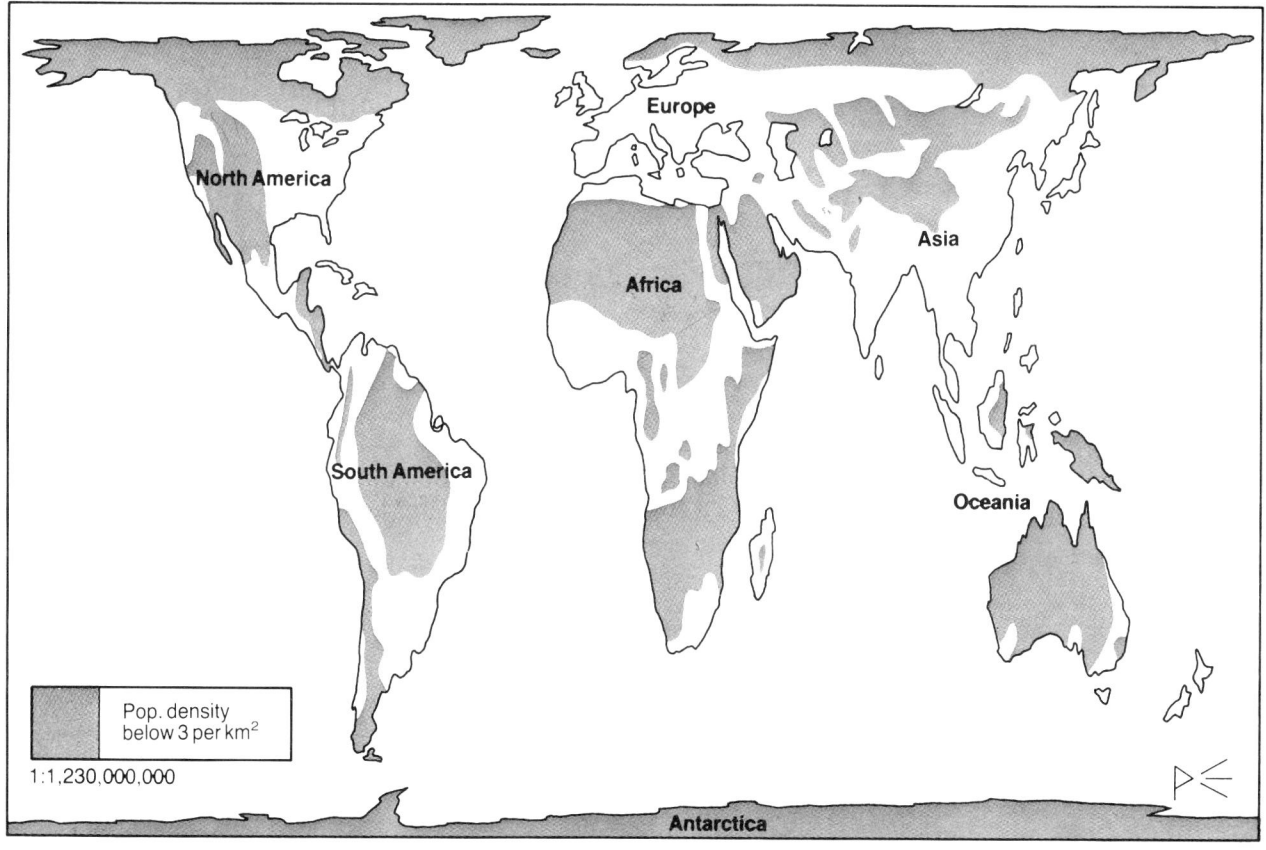

Europe

North America

Asia

Africa

South America

Oceania

Pop. density
below 3 per km²

1:1,230,000,000

Antarctica

Cold Lands

The photograph in Fig. 4 shows the **tundra**. It is early summer but there is still snow on the ground. These northern lands have very short summers and long cold winters as the graph for Aklavik shows (Fig. 5). There are no trees in this area but lichens, mosses, and some grasses and small flowering shrubs and plants can survive. Further north is the polar **ice-cap** where even these plants cannot grow because the snow and ice never melt. South of the tundra are forests but because it is still very cold only coniferous trees will grow there.

In the tundra, only the top 40-50 cm of soil may thaw during the summer. The soil below stays permanently frozen and this is known as **permafrost**. Although most of the tundra receives less than 200 mm of moisture during the year, the permafrost does not let it soak away. This allows plants to grow in what is often called a 'cold desert'.

With a growing season of around six weeks only a few species have adapted to the conditions. Most grow close to the ground where the air is warmer and there is some protection from the strong Arctic winds. For example the ground willow seldom grows above 10 cm high.

These plants provide an important source of food for many of the tundra animals. Some animals live there all the time. Shrews, voles and lemmings live in an undersnow world where temperatures seldom drop below

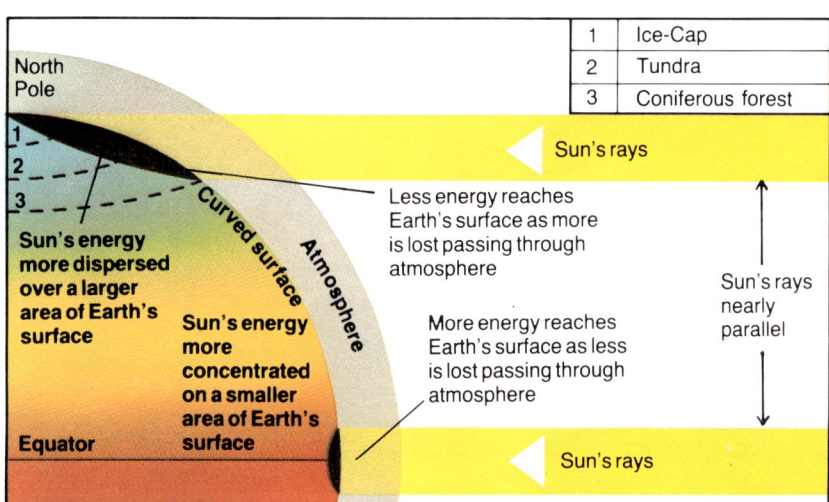

	1	Ice-Cap
	2	Tundra
	3	Coniferous forest

Figure 1

Figure 2

AVERAGE MONTHLY TEMPERATURES °C	JAN	FEB	MAR	APR	MAY	JUN	JUL	AUG	SEP	OCT	NOV	DEC
VERKHOYANSK	−50	−44	−32	−11	3	15	16	11	4	−15	−37	−45
MANCHESTER	5	5	6	8	13	15	17	16	14	11	7	5

−3°C. Others, such as the reindeer or caribou, travel north to the tundra each summer in search of fresh grazing as the snow begins to melt. They enjoy eating the lichens which grow there. Their large feet are well designed for digging through the snow in search of food and for walking on top of the snow and the spongy tundra ground.

But why is it so much colder as we travel farther away from the Equator towards the poles? The main reason is because different parts of the Earth receive different amounts of energy and light from the sun. Much of the sun's energy is lost as it passes through the Earth's atmosphere which is fortunate for us. If more reached Earth it would be too hot for life as we know it to exist! Fig. 1 shows why it is hotter at the Equator and colder at the poles.

When it is dark, energy from the sun does not reach the Earth's surface. This is why it is warmer during the day and cooler at night. The difference between the highest daytime and the lowest nighttime temperatures during 24 hours is the diurnal range.

Within the Arctic and Antarctic circles constant darkness and constant daylight are experienced at different times of the year. This happens because the Earth's axis, an imaginary line between the poles, is tilted. Fig. 3 shows the Earth in June when the Arctic has 24 hours of daylight. At this time of year tourists travel north beyond the Arctic circle to see the **midnight sun**. During the period of darkness it gets colder and colder. As Fig. 5 illustrates it is only in March, when the sun reappears, that temperatures in Aklavik slowly begin to rise.

1 With the help of Fig. 4 write a description of what you think the tundra is like. Try to include information on its vegetation, animal life and climate.

2 As the tundra receives so little moisture in the form of rain and snow, why does it become so spongy and swampy during the summer?

3 Fig. 2 gives average monthly temperatures for Verkhoyansk in the U.S.S.R. and Manchester in England.
(a) Draw line graphs for both of these places using the same scale.
(b) Compare your two graphs and describe how they differ.

4 Use Fig. 1 to explain why it becomes colder as you travel farther away from the Equator towards the poles.

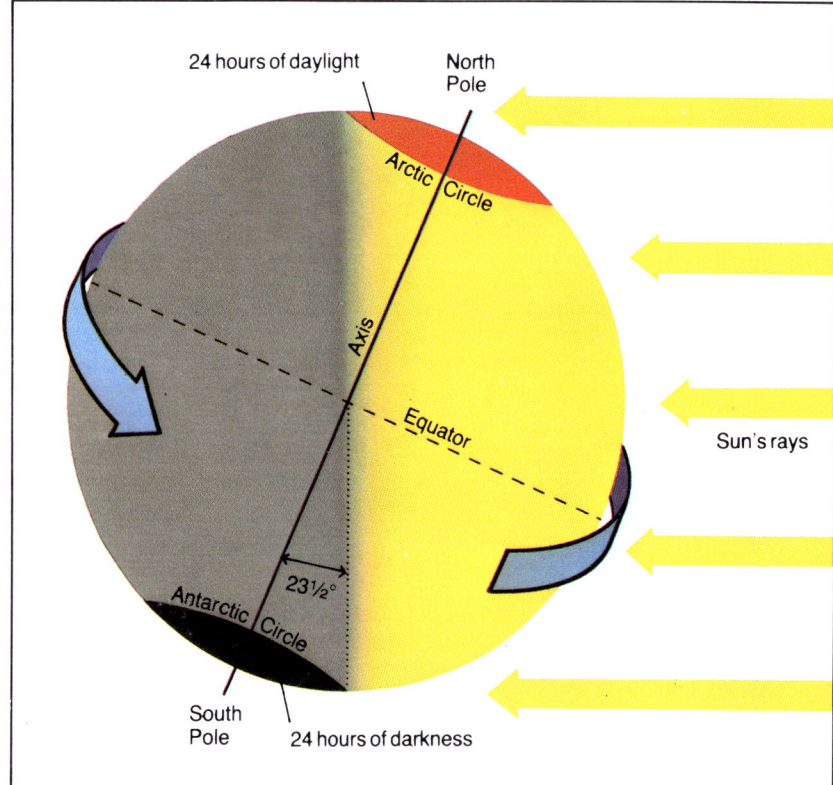

Figure 3

5 Wherever you live you are likely to notice a difference between the length of day and night at different times of the year. Describe the differences between June and December.

6 What do you think is meant by the midnight sun? Use an atlas to suggest which countries you could go to in order to see it in June.

7 Fig. 3 shows the Earth in June. Try to draw a similar diagram to show the Earth in December.

8 **Project Idea:** Many plants and animals are adapted for survival in the tundra. Try to find out how some of them survive. Include drawings if you wish.

Figure 4: A lake and tundra in late spring, 200 miles north of Churchill, Manitoba, Canada

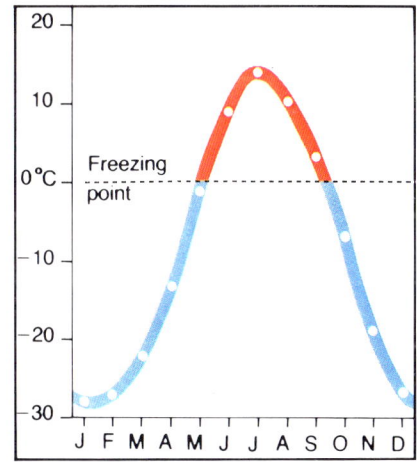

Figure 5

First Contacts – Explorers and Adventurers

Figure 1: This photo was taken during Scott's fatal Antarctic expedition of 1910-12

In the year 985 a Norse chieftain, Eric the Red, sailed west to Greenland with 400 Viking settlers. Why Eric called this new land 'green' is unclear. About 85% of the country is covered by an ice-sheet, which is over 3,000 m thick in places (see Fig. 2). Perhaps he thought the name would attract more settlers or maybe he only saw the area around the south-west coast where trees and grass do grow.

The Vikings from Norway were great explorers. They explained their polar adventures and expeditions in three ways.
1 To gain honour and praise by overcoming great dangers.
2 To increase knowledge and learning.
3 To search for wealth.
The same reasons still apply to explorers and adventurers a thousand years later!

In the sixteenth century sailors began the search for a way from Europe to the Pacific Ocean around the Arctic ice. They were unsuccessful. During 1845-7 Sir John Franklin with 128 officers and crew attempted to find the Northwest Passage. Scurvy, hunger, exhaustion and exposure to the cold all took their toll and the complete expedition perished. By the turn of the century a race for the North Pole was developing. On 6 April 1909, Robert E. Peary officially reached the North Pole.

In the south exploration had also been taking place. It was believed that somewhere there was a fertile southern continent. Following various reports of this mysterious land, James Cook finally crossed the Antarctic Circle in 1773. Although fog made visibility poor he reported a land of 'everlasting frigidness'.

Was this ice covered land one large continent? Was it a number of small islands? How thick was the ice? A lot was still not known and of course there was the South Pole to reach.

Ernest Shackleton nearly reached the South Pole in January 1909. At 88°23' south he was forced to turn back by 'a blinding, shrieking blizzard'.

The 'race to the pole' was left to Scott and Amundsen (Fig. 1). Temperatures of −56° C forced Amundsen to abandon his first attempt. He feared that Scott with his new motor sledges would reach the pole first. Amundsen set out again with 52 dogs and four well-equipped sledges. Twelve days later Scott set off – 300 km behind his rival. The sledges only lasted five days!

Amundsen reached the South Pole and raised the Norwegian flag. Scott was still 580 km away and manhauling his sledges. Shortages of food and fuel and generally poor organisation added to the disappointment of arriving a month after Amundsen. On the return journey, Scott and his remaining two companions died in their tent about 13th March.

1 Write down the 3 reasons for the Vikings' polar adventures. If you were planning an expedition explain which of these reasons would be most important to you?

2 The Greenland Vikings traded walrus tusk ivory with Europe in exchange for iron, timber, wine, glassware, and other luxury goods. What does this tell you about the available resources in Greenland?

3 After 500 years of living in Greenland the settlers suddenly disappeared. Were they killed by Eskimos from the north? Was there a sudden epidemic? Did they die from hunger? Archaelogists are still busy exploring the farm sites and hope to solve the mystery. What do you think might have happened to them? Write a short story in which you solve the mystery.

4 Copy the map of the Arctic (Fig. 2) and use different colours for the permanent ice, drift ice, sea and land. Then use an atlas to add the bays, straits, islands and seas

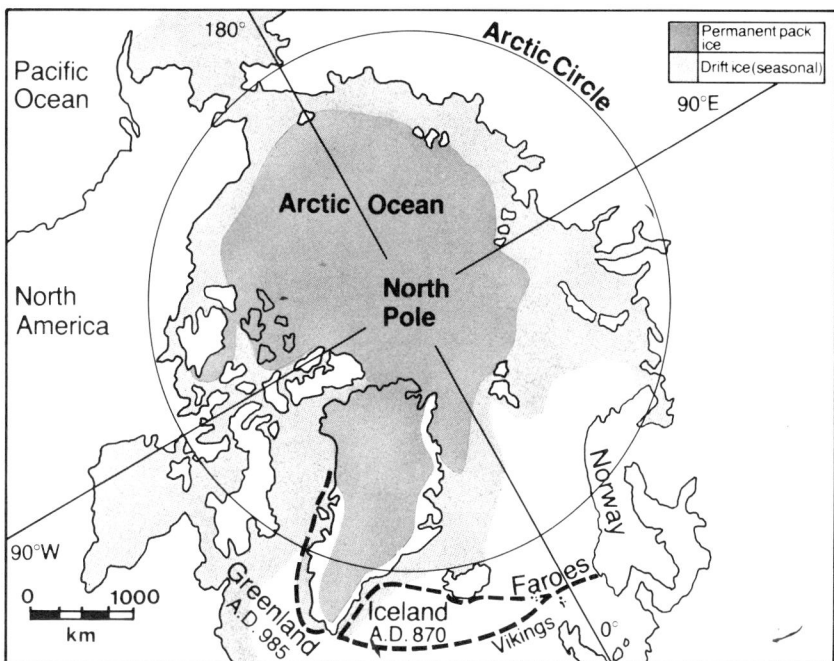

Figure 2: The Arctic

named after the following explorers: Frobisher, Hudson, Davis, Baffin, Barents and Bering.

5 Among the early visitors to the Antarctic were James Weddell, James Ross and Charles Wilkes. Match their names with place names at the letters A to D on the Antarctic map (Fig. 3).

6 Deep cracks in the ice (crevasses) covered with snow, rough, uneven ice and soft snow all make travel in the Antarctic difficult. Explain the problems each creates.

7 Use the information on Fig. 3 to work out how long it took Amundsen to reach the South Pole. If this was a journey of about 1,120 km, how far did they travel on average each day?

8 Use the dates and details provided, including those on Fig. 3, to write a brief account of the race to the South Pole.

9 **Project Idea:** It is difficult for most animals to live in the Arctic and Antarctic. However, there is food in the sea so that some animals like the penguin, seal and walrus can survive. Find out how they are adapted to polar life and draw pictures of them.

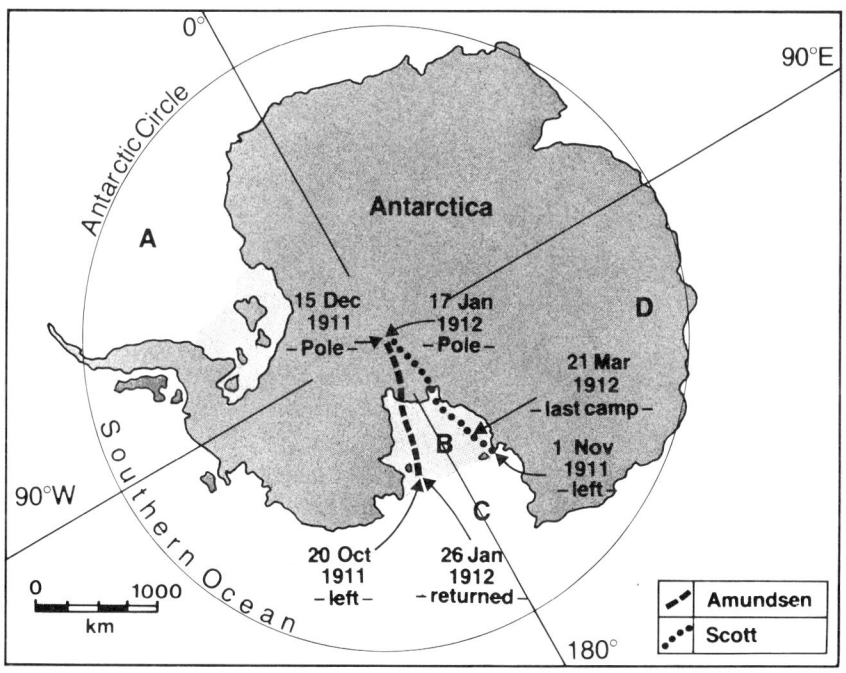

Figure 3: The Antarctic

11

Using the Resources – Trappers and the Fur Trade

Animals living in cold and mountainous regions have adapted to survive the harsh winters. People also have to adapt. Where farming is impossible people such as the Carrier Indians of Canada's Rocky Mountains have survived mainly by hunting, trapping and fishing. The skins and furs of the animals around them provided shelter and clothing.

Figure 1: Fort St. James, British Columbia

It was these furs that attracted outsiders to Canada's cold lands. By 1800 the fur trade had already spread west to the Rockies. Fort St. James was built in 1806 and operated by the Hudson's Bay Company. This was the trading centre of New Caledonia, a vast area between the Coast and Rocky Mountains (Fig. 2).

Trappers took their furs to the trade store where they were graded and valued. The beaver, marten, otter and muskrat pelts were then exchanged for supplies. In the early days only one trip was made each year to bring in supplies and take out furs. Harsh winters and isolation meant a lonely and hard life at the fort, making it the Siberia of the fur trade! By the 1930s the fur trade had declined and Fort St. James was abandoned.

1 Why were outsiders first attracted to cold lands such as the northern parts of the Rockies?

2 What difficulties did the trappers and traders have to overcome?

3 Look at the photo of Fort St. James (Fig. 1). What materials have been used for building? Explain why you think this is so.

4 (a) Copy the map of the area around Fort St. James (Fig. 2).
(b) Work out the distance of the journey from Prince George to Fort St. James.
(c) Describe the route and illustrate the different methods of transport used.
(d) The main market for furs was in Europe. Was Prince Rupert well situated for this? Explain why.

5 What effects, good and bad, do you think the fur trade had on this part of Canada?

6 **Project Idea:** Find out more about trappers and describe a typical year's work.

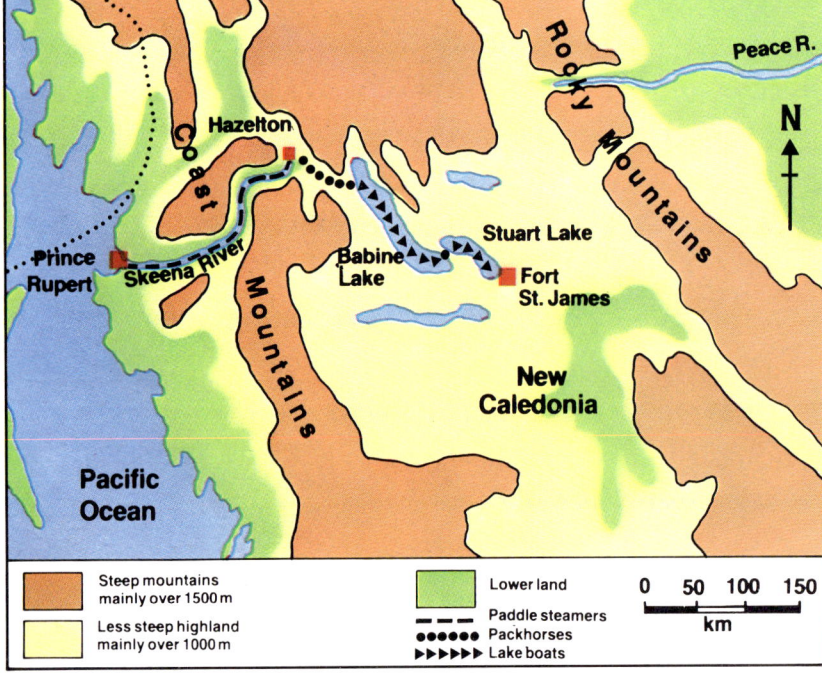

Figure 2

Steep mountains mainly over 1500 m
Less steep highland mainly over 1000 m
Lower land
Paddle steamers
Packhorses
Lake boats

0 50 100 150
km

Life of the Trapper

The trappers set out in mid-September just before the freeze-up. They had to carry the winter's supplies and their traps. Winter cabins were often primitive and cramped with a stove, traps, snowshoes and wet clothing plus the smell of damp leather. Outside was the endless forest with its white canopy of snow that deadened all sound. They worked their trapping lines throughout the winter. Toboggans piled with furs were dragged back over frozen lakes and rivers during April and May.

Grizzly!

Standing 3 m high and weighing 900 pounds, a full grown male grizzly is a magnificent animal (Fig. 3). It is also well adapted to cold lands with its thick fur coat.

Grizzlies are mainly **herbivorous**. They eat roots, berries, herbs and other plants. They will also eat meat when it is easily available. You can't be too fussy about your food in a cold, harsh environment!

Even so there is not enough food available during the winter, so the grizzlies **hibernate**, or sleep, from mid-November until April when they leave their dens.

They normally avoid people. If surprised they may attack, especially when protecting their young. To the Indians of North America they were godlike – proud, strong, fierce and independent – the guardian of the forest. Many early white settlers, however, thought they were a menace. Hunting them was a challenge. James Brewster shot over 150 grizzlies in the Canadian Rockies earlier this century.

The National Parks of Canada offer sanctuary to wildlife and protection to the natural environment. They are for the 'benefit, education and enjoyment of the Canadian people'. They are not for the benefit of the grizzly. Some bears are hit and killed by vehicles, others are shot to protect visitors.

More people in the parks means more rubbish. Food waste found near settlements and camp sites attracts the grizzly who then becomes a threat to human safety. The bear may be tranquilised and taken to an isolated part of the park. If it returns it will probably be shot. As more people explore wilderness areas, so the future of animals like the grizzly is threatened.

1 Explain three ways in which the grizzly is well adapted to live in a cold environment.

2 (a) How and why did the Indians and white settlers differ in their opinions of the grizzly?
(b) James Brewster was proud of his achievement. What is your opinion of what he did?

3 (a) Why were the Canadian National Parks set up?
(b) Have the parks helped the grizzly? Explain your answer.

4 In what ways do human activities now pose a threat to the survival of the grizzly bear?

5 **Project Idea:** Find out more about hibernation. Which other animals do it and why?

Figure 3: Signs in French and English (right) warn tourists in Canadian National Parks against grizzly bears (above)

Peoples of the Arctic – The Eskimos

No one really knows where the Eskimos, or Inuit as they call themselves, came from. They may have originated in Siberia, entering North America some 50,000 years ago. It seems strange to us that they should have chosen to live in an area where we would find it so difficult to survive. However, they do seem to have chosen to live there rather than been forced to do so by some natural disaster or by human enemies.

Traditional Eskimo societies had the reputation for being cheerful, generous and friendly. To be a good hunter and to help the community was far more important than the accumulation of personal wealth. Their homes, made of earth, skins, stone, or snow and ice, were designed to keep in the heat. The parkas which they wore were loose-fitting to allow body heat to circulate freely. By loosening the neck excess heat could escape to avoid the dangers of sweating in below freezing temperatures.

Figure 1: An Eskimo family in Polly Bay, Northwest Territories

Fishing and hunting provided all of their needs. For example, the caribou gave them meat to eat, skins for tents and clothes (Fig. 1), fat to burn in lamps and bones for making tools and ornaments.

About 300 years ago they came into contact with the white traders of the Hudson's Bay Company. Many Eskimos were encouraged to become fur traders. Unfortunately their ability to survive in the harsh climate did not protect them against the white man's diseases, such as measles, which often proved fatal.

Today there are about 95,000 Eskimos – less than a full house at Wembley Stadium! Snowmobiles, rifles and outboard motor boats have all done much to change their way of life during the last thirty to forty years. Up until the late 1950s the Eskimos around Hudson Bay were still nomadic hunters. Now most of them live in permanent settlements built by the government along the coast (Fig. 2). They have become increasingly dependant upon supply ships which call during the summer. These bring prefabricated wooden houses, fuel oil, sweets, video cassettes, and many other 'new' products. It is difficult to decide whether the changes have been good or bad.

Figure 2: A modern Eskimo settlement in Inuvik, Northwest Territories

The government provides houses, medical care, and unemployment assistance. Rifles and snowmobiles make hunting easier. Aeroplanes arrive to recruit seasonal workers for mining exploration. Silver, zinc, copper, lead, iron, uranium and nickel have attracted the large mining companies into the frozen north.

For some these changes have brought unemployment and alcoholism. Children leave their families to go to school and many do not learn the old, traditional survival skills. Some skills have been adapted. Eskimo carvings have become another source of income. Personal wealth has become more important to many of the younger people. They want to buy cars and televisions and other symbols of the Western life style. Perhaps some changes have happened too fast?

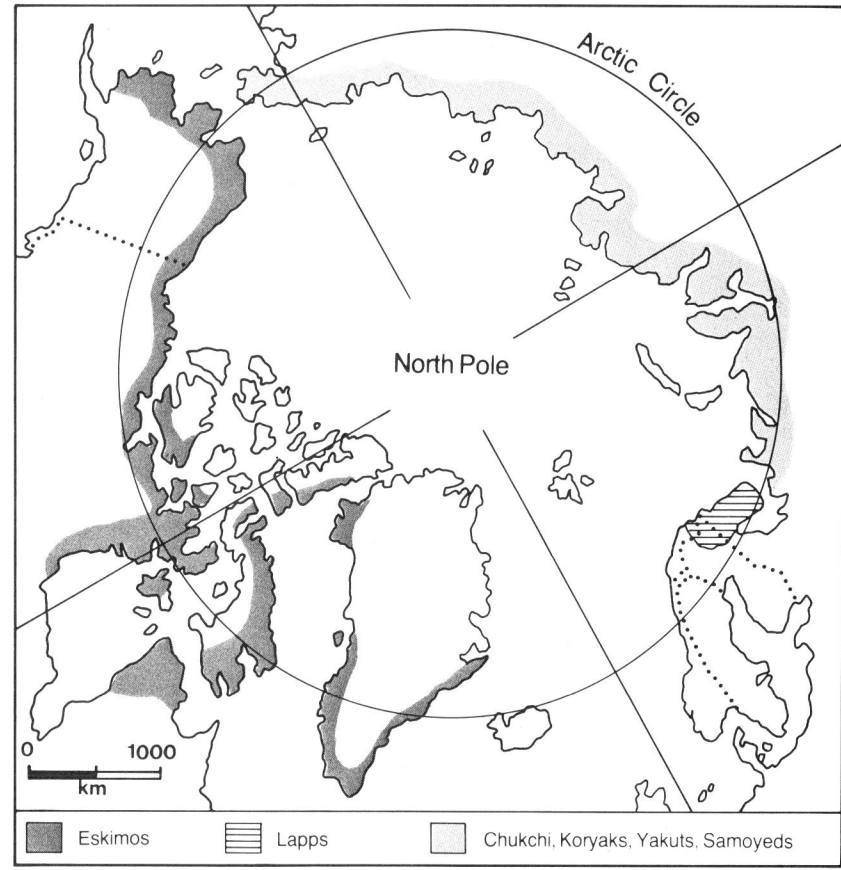

Figure 3: Peoples of the Arctic

1 Traditional Eskimo lifestyle (Fig. 4) depended on dog sledges, spears, harpoons, kayaks and bows and arrows.
(a) What have replaced these?
(b) What effect do you think hunting with rifles has had on the size of the caribou herds? Explain your answer.
(c) Snowmobiles are now more common than dog sledges — although the dogs do not break down in bad weather! What do you think are the advantages and disadvantages of both types of transport?

2 (a) Why have other people been attracted to these cold, northern lands?
(b) Describe the changes which have taken place as a result of greater contact with people from other cultures.
(c) Would you say that these changes have been good or bad for the Eskimos? Use examples to explain your answer.

3 The Eskimos are not the only group of people who live within the Arctic Circle. Fig. 3 shows where other groups live. Draw the map and use an atlas to add the names of the countries in which they live.

4 To the west of Hudson Bay is a region called Keewatin. Its population of about 4,500 live in an area of 595,000 km². Work out the density of population (population ÷ area). Is this high or low density? (UK is 230 per km²).

5 Make a list of the survival skills you would need to exist in the tundra plains.

Figure 4: Traditional Eskimo hunting methods are shown on this engraved walrus tusk

Extracting the Wealth – Oil in Alaska

Gold! In 1897-8 thousands of miners headed north in the Klondike Gold Rush (Fig. 1). The desire for wealth overcomes many hardships. Within three years Dawson City had grown into a town of 30,000. When the gold ran out most people left. By 1961 Dawson City had a population of just 881.

The Arctic lands are rich in mineral wealth. Silver, copper, uranium, zinc and many other deposits are known to exist. Today in Alaska it is oil – black gold – which has attracted people to the frozen north. In 1963 the largest oil field ever discovered in North America was found around Prudhoe Bay on Alaska's northern coastline (Fig. 1).

There is plenty of oil and gas there, but getting to it has not been easy. Working within the Arctic Circle creates a number of

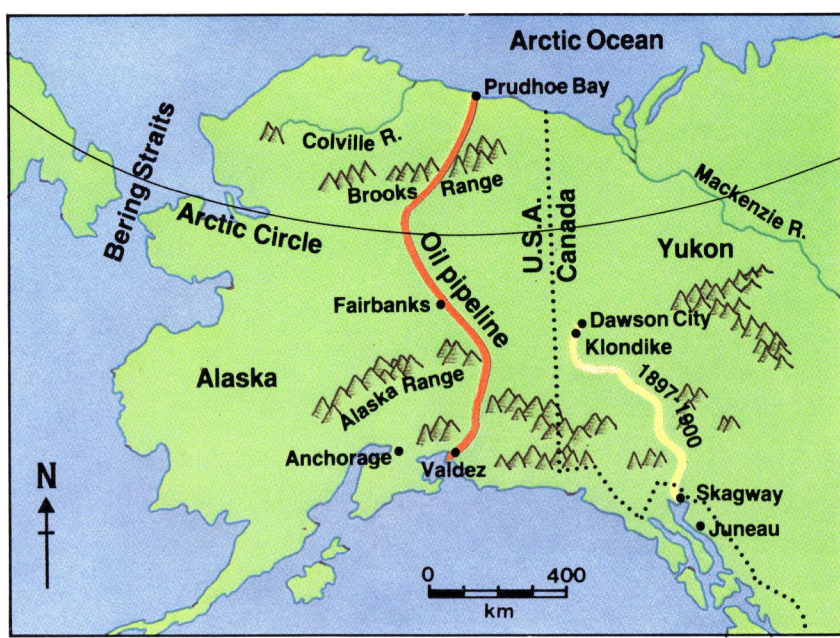

Figure 1: Alaska, showing the route of the pipeline

difficulties. In 1963 Prudhoe Bay had no road or rail links. The coast is only ice-free for six weeks of the year. In mid-winter there are eight weeks of total darkness. Temperatures drop to −51°C. Equipment freezes and even steel becomes brittle. **Permafrost** makes building difficult.

Permafrost is ground which is always frozen. Above the frozen ground is a thin **active layer** of about 45 cm which melts during the summer. If the permafrost is made to melt then buildings and other structures may collapse. To stop this, all buildings are raised on pilings over gravel pads. This allows air to circulate and stops extra warmth reaching the frozen ground.

The oil companies have overcome all of these problems but it cost a lot of money and took a long time. British Petroleum (BP) is one of the companies operating around Prudhoe Bay. Their first equipment was taken by road to the Great Slave Lake. Then down the Mackenzie River to the Arctic Ocean and along the coast. In 1968 a route from Anchorage via

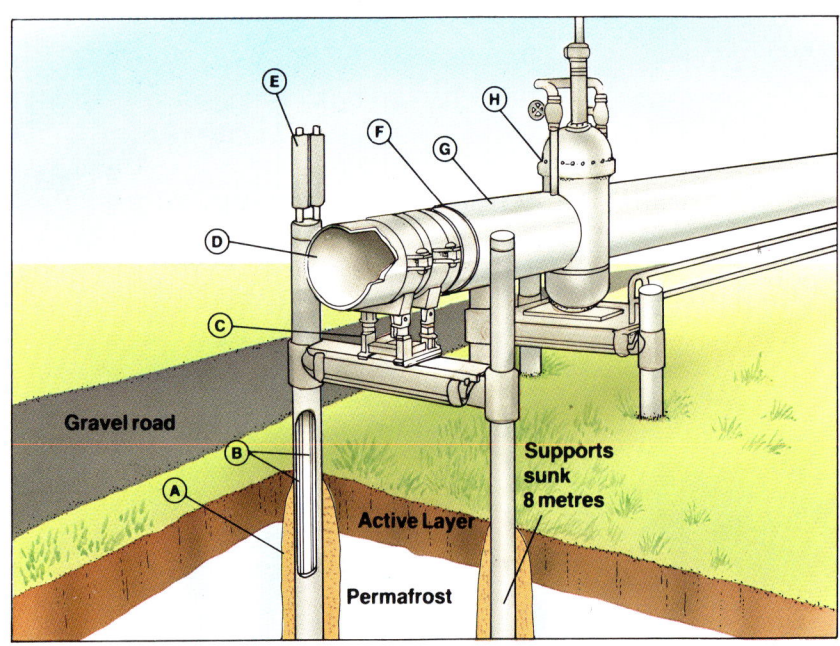

Figure 2: The pipeline

16

the Bering Strait was used. Two drilling rigs were even flown in and reassembled. The aircraft cost £250,000 a month to operate.

Life at Prudhoe Bay is difficult and often unpleasant. The cold wind blowing from the Arctic brings air temperatures down to −80°C. To reduce boredom the camp has an indoor swimming pool, an enclosed temperature-controlled sports field, video television, a cinema, good food, and many other opportunities for recreation. Skilled craftsmen and labourers can earn very high wages.

Drilling at low temperatures was a problem. Steel snapped, lubricants froze and steam hoses were needed to unfreeze equipment. Permafrost demanded new drilling methods. Finally the oil companies had to find a way of carrying the oil. There were many suggestions – build a railway, use huge ocean-going tankers or giant sledges. The final decision was to construct a 1,275 km pipeline to Valdez (Fig. 3). By 1969 about £50 m worth of pipes were stacked at Valdez, Fairbanks and Prudhoe Bay. They remained untouched for the next four years.

The delay was due to fears that the pipeline would damage the delicate **tundra** environment. The U.S. government finally gave the go-ahead and by 1975 there were over 20,000 people at work. In 1977 the first oil reached Valdez having crossed three mountain ranges (Fig. 1), 600 streams and rivers and an area which suffers from earthquakes. It cost almost £4,000 m to build.

Figure 3: Part of the Alaskan pipeline near Prudhoe Bay, Alaska

1 Drilling at Prudhoe Bay.
(a) Use an atlas to draw a map showing the routes used to take in equipment and supplies.
(b) Explain why such long and expensive routes were used.
(c) Describe the problems faced by the drilling teams.

2 Living at Prudhoe Bay.
(a) What is it like during the winter months in northern Alaska?
(b) How is life made more pleasant and what is special about the buildings?
(c) Why do you think people go to work in an area like this? Would you expect them to stay for long?

3 Building the pipeline. Special problems were created by the permafrost and the risk of earthquakes. Figs. 2 and 3 show how these were overcome.
(a) Draw your own simpler version of Fig. 3 and add the following labels.
A Frozen sand and water.
B Liquid ammonia keeps soil frozen.

C 'Shoes' allow pipe to slide on support beam in case of 'quake or expansion and contraction.
D 120 cm steel pipe.
E Radiator allows ammonia to lose heat. Cooled ammonia runs back down pipe.
F 10 cm thick fibreglass insulation keeps oil above 25°C.
G Outer steel casing.
H Safety valve designed to close in four minutes.
(b) Why do you think it is so important to keep the supports cold and the oil warm?
(c) Copy Fig. 1 and then explain why it cost so much to build.

4 **Project Idea:** The **environmentalists** tried to stop the building of the pipeline. They thought it would interfere with wildlife and that oil spills could damage the area. Special valves should close within four minutes but 15,000 barrels of oil could still escape. Using any information you can find, prepare a case either *for* or *against* the building of the pipeline.

Building a Pipeline

The map in Fig. 2 shows an imaginary area around the Arctic Circle. Oil has been found and you have the job of planning and constructing a pipeline to carry it to a port on the south coast. Building a pipeline in an area like this is difficult. Some land is mountainous, some affected by earthquakes, some by permafrost. The costs will change depending on what the land is like. Fig. 1 shows the costs involved. They include research, building roads, buying equipment, transporting materials, paying wages and preparing the ground.

Planning the Pipeline
Your first job is to plan the pipeline. Your aim is to choose a route from the oilfield (O) to one of the ports (A, B, or C). You may pass through a square vertically, horizontally or diagonally. The cost for developing the squares is shown in Fig. 1 plus extra costs for river crossings and burying the pipeline to allow migrating animals to pass freely.

1 Copy out the table (Fig. 1).

2 Work out the cheapest route from the oilfield to one of the ports.

3 Complete the table by filling in the number of squares or crossings of each type.

4 Work out your total estimated costs. If they are over £4,000 m then you must work out another route.

5 If it takes an average of two months to construct each square, work out your estimated construction time.

A number of problems are likely to interfere with your plans. Extra costs, delays and accidents cannot be included in your original estimates.

Building the Pipeline
Start building from the port you have selected. Move forward one square at a time. Throw a dice as you move into each square. Scores of 1, 2, 4 or 5 allow you to move on with no extra costs or other difficulties.

If you throw 3 or 6 you must roll the dice again and carry out one of the following, depending on your score.

1 Equipment breaks down due to sub-zero temperatures. Add £50 million and 1 month.

2 Pipes not welded correctly, all joints must be re-welded. Go back 3 squares.

3 Conservationists' fears of damage to the environment result in delays. Add £20 m and 4 months.

4 Pipes damaged in transit. Go back one square.

5 Permafrost melts and foundations collapse. Add £50 m and go back 3 squares.

6 Progress as normal.

Record all of your costs as you build the pipeline and total up your actual costs. Do the same with the time.

Conclusions
With a project of this sort there is a combination of skill and chance. In the game you used your skill in selecting the route. The dice represented the chance factors.

1 Expain how you worked out the route to follow.

2 Compare your estimated costs and time with the actual costs and time. How much more did it cost and how much longer did it take?

3 Write an account explaining the reasons for your extra costs and time.

Figure 1

PLANNING THE PIPELINE

Key	Conditions	Cost per sq.	No. Squares	Cost
	Mountains	£200 m		£
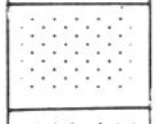	Earthquake zone	£200 m		£
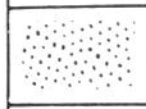	Permafrost	£100 m		£
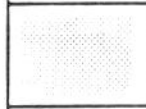	Non-permafrost	£50 m		£
	River crossing	£100 m		£
	Migratory route	£250 m		£
	Total estimated time		months	
	Total estimated cost			£

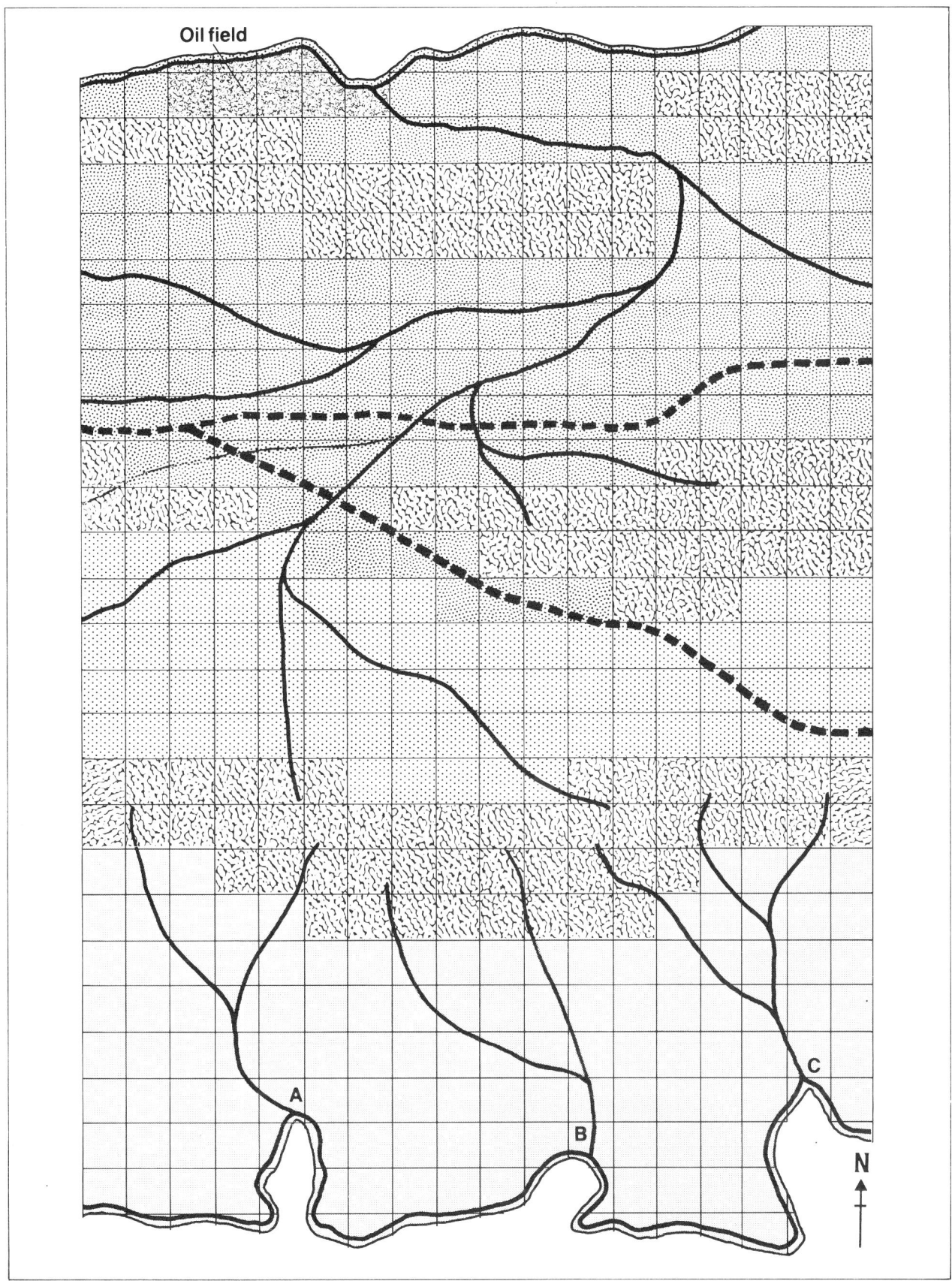

Oil field

Figure 2

Cold Mountain Environments

Snow and ice near the Equator? The photograph (Fig. 1) shows Mt. Kilimanjaro. It is only about 300 km south of the Equator. It has an altitude, or height above sea level, of around 5,895 m. The photograph clearly shows that it is very cold at the summit.

It is always cold at the top of high mountains. This is because for every 200 m you go up the temperature of the air around you falls by 1°C. So the climate found at the top of a mountain will be very different from the climate found at the bottom (Fig. 2). The descent from summit to rainforest on Kilimanjaro is like travelling from the Arctic to the Equator in just 3,000 m. Above the **permanent snow line** the snow and ice never melt. On Kilimanjaro, near the Equator, the permanent snow line is up at 5,200 m above sea level. At the North and South Poles the climate is much colder. There is permanent snow and ice right down to sea level. In very cold climates huge quantities of ice

Figure 1: Mt. Kilimanjaro in Tanzania, the highest peak in Africa

may build up in mountain valleys to form **glaciers**. The ice in a glacier moves slowly downhill. Trapped at the bottom and sides of the ice are rocks and boulders. As the glacier moves it acts like a huge block of sandpaper. Gradually it wears away the floor and sides of its valley making it wider and deeper. This wearing away process is called **erosion**.

Fig. 3 shows what a mountain valley looks like when it is filled by a glacier. The diagram also shows what the valley would look like if all the ice was to melt. Notice how its flat floor and steep sides make it a **U-shaped valley**. Notice too that at the front, or snout, of the glacier the ice is melting. This is because it is warmer lower down the valley. High up in the mountains the ice gouges out large rock basins called **corries**. These act as reservoirs of ice which help to feed the glaciers moving down the mountain valleys. The land under the ice is worn smooth. Above the ice though the land is left jagged and pointed. This is because of a process called freeze-thaw. During the day, when it is warmer, water collects in cracks in the rock. Then at night, when it becomes colder, the water freezes. When it freezes it expands and the ice in the cracks

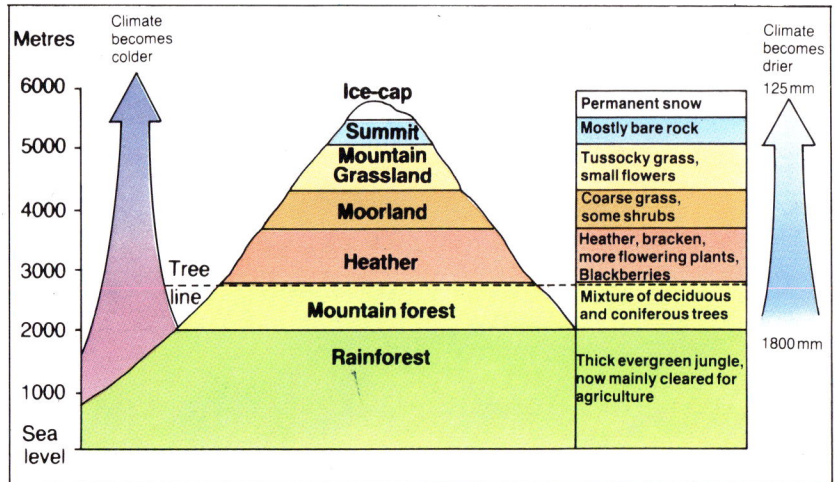

Figure 2: Climate and vegetation zones on Mt. Kilimanjaro

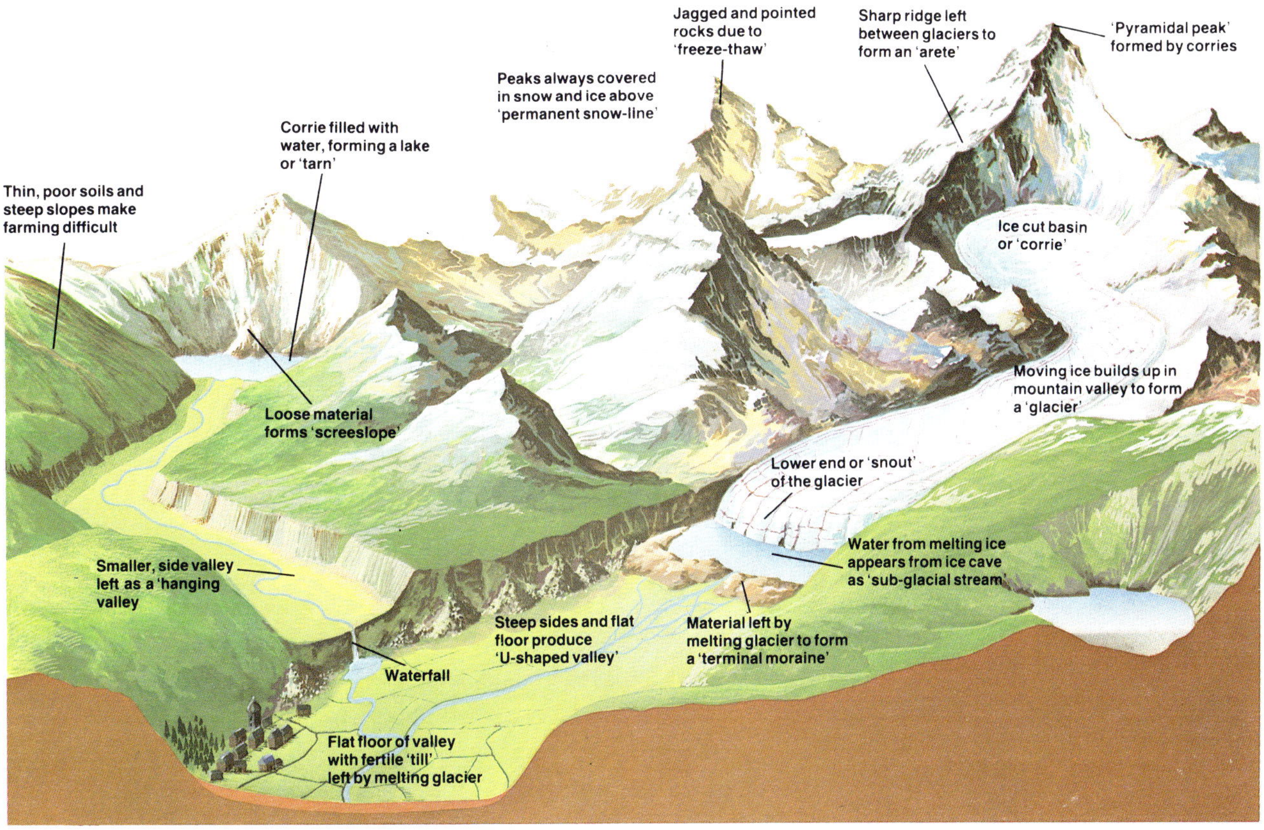
Jagged and pointed rocks due to 'freeze-thaw'
Sharp ridge left between glaciers to form an 'arete'
'Pyramidal peak' formed by corries
Peaks always covered in snow and ice above 'permanent snow-line'
Corrie filled with water, forming a lake or 'tarn'
Thin, poor soils and steep slopes make farming difficult
Ice cut basin or 'corrie'
Moving ice builds up in mountain valley to form a 'glacier'
Loose material forms 'screeslope'
Lower end or 'snout' of the glacier
Water from melting ice appears from ice cave as 'sub-glacial stream'
Smaller, side valley left as a 'hanging valley
Steep sides and flat floor produce 'U-shaped valley'
Material left by melting glacier to form a 'terminal moraine'
Waterfall
Flat floor of valley with fertile 'till' left by melting glacier

Figure 3: During and after glaciation in the mountains

forces the rock apart. If this freezing and thawing is repeated many times pieces of rock are broken off. The land is left looking jagged and sharp.

1 Explain why altitude makes it difficult for mountaineers to decide what clothing to take with them on an expedition.

2 (a) What is meant by the permanent snow line?
(b) Why is there permanent snow and ice on the top of Mt. Kilimanjaro even though it is so close to the Equator?

3 Use Fig. 2 to describe the changes you would see around you as you climbed Kilimanjaro.

4 What is the front of the glacier called? What do you think happens to it in a) warmer weather; b) colder weather?

5 Draw a simple diagram of a valley that has been shaped by a glacier. What letter is used to describe the valley shape?

6 Use Fig. 3 to help you to answer these questions about glaciers and the valleys they form:
(a) What is the name given to the material left by the melting glacier? Where is most of it found?
(b) During the summer some of the glacier ice melts. Why is this and what happens to the melt-water?
(c) What are hanging valleys? Suggest how they were formed.

7 Look at the land above the glacier in Fig. 3:
(a) What process helps to break up the rocks on the mountains above the ice? In your own words explain what happens.
(b) What are the sharp ridges left between two glaciers called?
(c) What happens to the shape of a mountain if the ice gouges out huge corries all around it?

8 The following are some of the highest mountain ranges in the world: *Alaska, Alps, Andes, Atlas, Caucasus, Coast, Ethiopian Highlands, Himalaya, Hindu Kush, Karakoram, Pyrenees, Rocky, Sierra Madre, Southern Alps, Zagros.*
(a) Find these mountains in your atlas and mark them on your own copy of a world map.
(b) Draw and then complete a table by adding the name and height of the major peak and the countries in which the mountain range is found.

9 In Scotland, Fort William is just above sea level. If it has an average temperature of 8°C at what height should the permanent snow line be found? Use your atlas to find out if a permanent snow line will occur in Scotland. Explain your decision.

Up in the Mountains – Switzerland

Switzerland is a country of mountains. A quarter of it is steep or snow covered. This means that most people live in the lower region between the Alps and Jura mountains (Fig. 2). It is here that most people live and here that most farming and industry can be found.

In the Alps people live in villages in the valleys. Most villages are found on the south-facing slopes which receive more sunshine. Farming has never been easy. In the past, the Alpine farmers would take their cattle up the mountain sides as the snow melted in early June. The cattle would graze on the spring **alp** or mountain pasture and then move up higher to the summer alp. Fig. 1 shows one of these pastures.

The farmer and his family would stay with the cattle, living in a simple wooden shelter. Milk was taken down to the creamery in the village. Hay was also cut and carried down to the farm in the valley. This was used to feed the cattle during the long winter. At the end of September the cattle would be brought down the mountain to spend the winter in their stalls.

Some farming does still take place using these methods. Most of the mountain villages now depend increasingly on tourism for their livelihood. The beautiful scenery attracts visitors at all times of the year. The regular snow cover on the mountain slopes makes Switzerland an important centre for winter sports.

Figure 1: Mountain pasture near the Swiss village of Grindelwald

The Alps are a winter paradise. They offer relaxing holidays in a healthy climate, pure mountain air, sunshine, glittering snow and wonderful peace. The great variety of fine downhill ski-runs are suitable for both beginners and experts. There are many other sports: cross-country skiing, riding, tobogganing, ice-skating, skibob, skiwalking and even swimming. Some of these can be seen in the photos below and at the bottom of the opposite page.

Above: A cable car in the Swiss Alps
Left: Cross-country skiing
Right: A bobsleigh run at St Moritz

1 Fig. 2 shows the nine largest towns in Switzerland.
(a) What do they all have in common?
(b) About three-quarters of Switzerland's population live between the Jura and Alps. Why do so many people live in such a small area of the country?

2 Make a copy of Fig. 2.
(a) Shade in the land over 700 m brown and the lower land green.
(b) Use your atlas to name as many of the lakes as you can.
(c) Use your atlas to mark and name these important tourist resorts: Interlaken, St Moritz, Davos.

3 Farming in the mountains needed a special kind of agriculture.
(a) Why was the alp so important to Swiss farmers?
(b) Why did farmers not keep their cattle on the mountain pastures all year?
(c) Would you say this was a hard or an easy way of life for farmers and their families? Explain your answer.

4 Tourism has offered a new way of life to many people living in the Alpine valleys. Imagine you live in

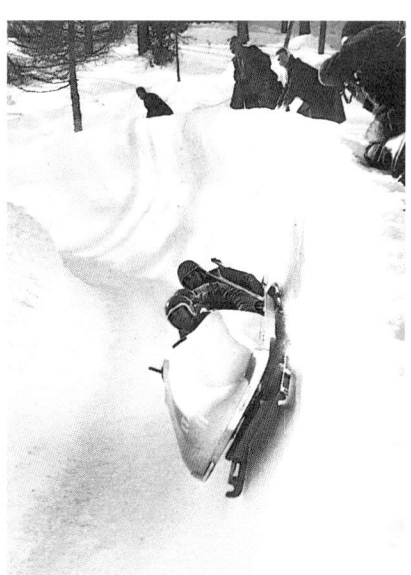

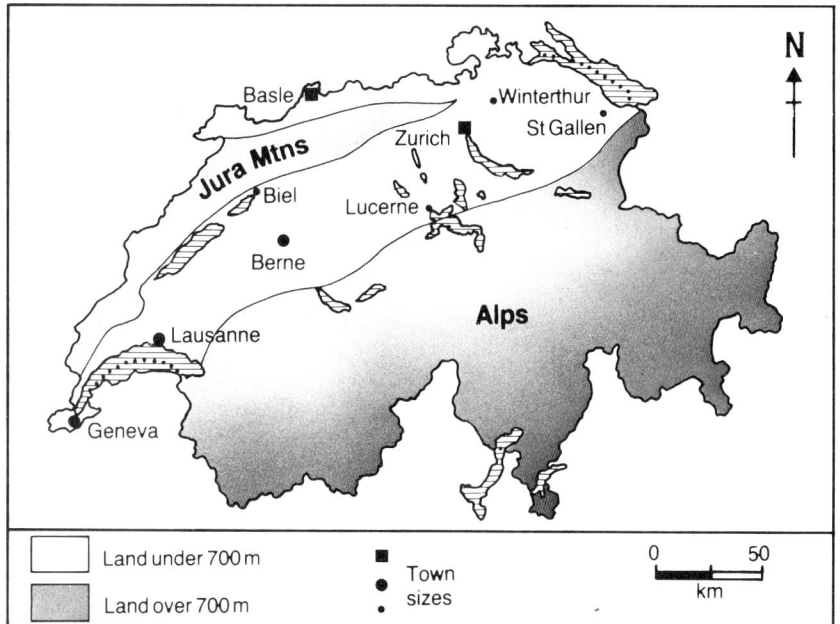

Figure 2: Switzerland

an area like this and describe the changes which have taken place.

5 In your own words explain what attracts visitors to the Swiss Alps.

6 Fig. 3 shows where most of Switzerland's visitors came from during the winter season 1981/82. The 'comparative score' relates the number of visitors to the total number of people in their countries (the larger the score, the higher the % of the country's population visiting Switzerland).
(a) On your own map of Europe use the 'comparative scores' to colour in the countries as follows:

Under 25	Green
25 – 75	Yellow
Over 75	Red
Switzerland	Black

(b) What do you notice about the countries you have coloured green?
(c) Austria, Italy and France are all very close to Switzerland but have a lower score than West Germany. Look at a physical map of Europe and try to suggest why this may be so.
(d) Some European countries

have not been coloured. Try to find out what they all have in common.

7 **Project Idea:** Find out more about the different types of winter sports.

Country	Visitors	Comparative Score
Austria	53,000	71
Belgium	95,000	97
Denmark	14,000	30
Finland	10,500	22
France	248,000	47
Greece	20,500	23
Italy	172,000	31
Irish Republic	5,000	17
Luxembourg	8,000	267
Netherlands	95,500	71
Norway	9,500	23
Portugal	13,500	15
Spain	46,500	23
Sweden	35,000	43
Turkey	24,000	8
U.K.	183,000	33
West Germany	742,000	120
Yugoslavia	20,000	10

Comparative Score: Based on the % of each country's population that visits Switzerland. e.g. 0.71% of Austria's population visited Switzerland, giving a score of 71.

Figure 3: Visitors to Switzerland during the winter season 1981-82

Up in the Mountains – Changes in Nepal

Standing on top of the world. That is how Edmund Hillary and Tenzing Norgay must have felt on 29 May 1953. They had reached the summit of Mt. Everest, the world's highest mountain.

The expedition approached Everest from Kathmandu in Nepal. Earlier climbs had to be attempted from the north as Nepal only opened its frontiers to outsiders in 1950. Since then more and more trekkers and climbers have visited the country. There were 4,000 in 1971 and 20,000 in 1981. Early visitors to Everest had to make an overland journey of 280 km from Kathmandu. It took about 10 days. Now they can fly from Kathmandu to the foothills in 30 minutes!

A Sherpa woman weaving

Figure 1: A trekkers' camp in the Annapurna region of Nepal

The Himalayas are a 'fragile' environment. It takes a long while for plants to grow on the mountain slopes. Soils are generally thin and easily damaged. Rainwater running downhill over exposed soil can wash it away. For example it takes over 40 years for a tree to grow. Demand for firewood and building timber has left some slopes bare and exposed to erosion. In the Khumbu Glacier Valley on the route to Everest there is hardly a juniper tree left.

The Sagarmatha National Park was created in 1976. It contains three of the world's highest mountains. It is hoped that it will protect one of the most popular areas of the Himalayas. The problem is too many people using limited resources. The delicate balance that the Sherpa people had with nature has been upset by the demands of the trekkers. The increased demand for wood has meant that the forests have been badly damaged in the Everest area. The Sagarmatha National Park rules do not allow 'green' wood to be cut. Only dead trees can officially be used. The 2,500 Sherpas within the new park understand the dangers of creating a treeless desert. They are worried, though, that regulations will restrict both firewood supplies and yak grazing pastures.

Before the trekkers and climbers arrived the Sherpas in each village had a forest guardian. It was up to him to prevent over-cutting. There was a harmony between people and the land.

Today, employment as high-altitude porters is important business for the Sherpas (Fig. 1). People not used to high altitudes suffer from mountain sickness so the Sherpa and his yak are in great demand. They carry trade goods, fuel, and expedition equipment. In some villages the money spent by climbers and trekkers has provided an important income for local people. The men are often away for many months. Communities have lost their sense of unity. The divorce rate has risen.

1 Use your atlas to draw a sketch map of Nepal. Mark on Mt. Everest, Annapurna, Kathmandu and the neighbouring countries. How high is Mt. Everest?

Figure 2: Terraced fields near a Sherpa village

2 Suggest reasons for the increase in the number of visitors to the Everest region in recent years.

3 The Sherpas have **terraced** the hillsides (Fig. 2). They grow crops such as barley and potatoes in their small fields surrounded with stone walls.
(a) Terraces are like shallow steps. Suggest why people farming hillsides go to all the bother of constructing them.
(b) Why do you think the Sherpas use stone walls and not hedges or wooden fences?

4 (a) Why has the arrival of so many more visitors resulted in the loss of trees in the Everest area?
(b) Why is the removal of trees in mountain regions of such great concern?
(c) How did the Sherpas control the use of wood before the visitors arrived?
(d) In your own words try to explain why the Sagarmatha

National Park was set up.
(e) Why do many local Sherpas object to the park?
(f) Reforestation, the planting of new trees, is now under way. Why will it be a long time before it makes much difference to the landscape?

5 The Himalayas is a *fragile environment* – explain what you think this means.

6 Write an account explaining what you think are the good and bad effects of recent development in Nepal.

7 Draw a sketch of the area shown in Fig. 2. Add the following labels: pyramidal peak; permanent snow; small terraced fields; farmers' homes.

8 **Project Idea:** Find out why mountain climbing is both difficult and dangerous in the Himalayas. Why do people do it?

Hot Lands

'We entered the dreaded black and chill forest called Mitamba, bidding farewell to sunshine and brightness... Down the boles and branches, creepers and vegetable cords, the moisture trickled and fell on us. Overhead the widespreading branches absolutely shut out daylight so that we marched in twilight.'

(Henry M. Stanley, *Through the Dark Continent*, 1876.)

'... I had felt as though the sun were burning a hole through my skull, thickly wrapped in a headcloth though it was.'

(Geoffrey Moorhouse, *The Fearful Void*, 1974.)

The hottest areas of the world are around the Equator – Fig. 1 on page 8 explains why this is so. More of the sun's energy reaches the Earth's surface near the Equator, and then it has to heat a smaller area of land than at the poles. The hot lands extend north and south of the Equator to just beyond the tropics of Cancer and Capricorn. These hot lands are often called the tropics, or tropical zone.

Within the tropics there is a wide range of different climates – nearly all are hot, but some are hot and very wet, while others are hot and very dry.

As Fig. 1 shows, hot and wet climates are found along the Equator. Moving away from the Equator the climate becomes increasingly drier. This explains why the **equatorial rainforests**, where plants grow quickly and well, are usually found along the Equator. It also explains why the tropical **deserts** occur along the tropics of Cancer and Capricorn. It is easy to explain why the tropics are hot, but less easy to explain why some parts are wet while other parts are dry. It is all to do with what is happening to the air at different places – as Fig. 2 explains. Air that is rising is being cooled, and when air is cooled it is more likely to form clouds and rain. Air that is sinking is being warmed and is less likely to form clouds and rain.

In some places the air is affected by cold ocean currents. Air is cooled as it blows over the cold current – and then warmed again as it reaches the land. This means that it is unlikely to form clouds and rain, and this is why deserts like the Atacama in South America are very dry indeed.

The crop of this farm in Rajasthan, India, has been destroyed by drought

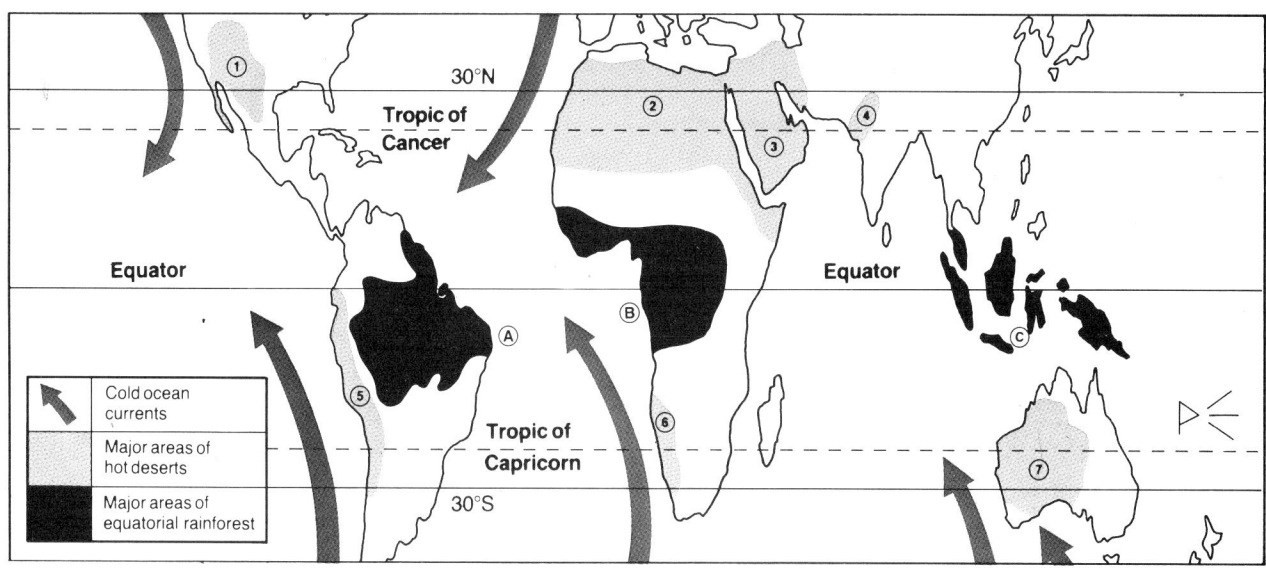

Figure 1: Equatorial rainforests, hot deserts and cold ocean currents

1 (a) Transfer the information from Fig. 1 onto your own copy of a world map.
(b) Use your atlas to pair the following deserts with the numbers 1 to 7: Arabian; Atacama; Great Australian; Kalahari/Namib; Sahara; Sonora; Thar.
(c) Use your atlas to pair the following rainforests with the letters A to C: Amazon Basin; Indonesia/Malaysia/New Guinea; Zaïre Basin.

2 Draw Fig. 2 and then write down what you think is the correct version of the following statements.
(a) Air rises in areas of *high/low* pressure.
(b) When air is warmed it is *more/less* likely to cause rain.
(c) The wettest parts of the tropics have *high/low* pressure.
(d) Tropical deserts are found where air *rises/sinks*.
(e) *Rainforests/deserts* are found along the Equator.

3 Look at Fig. 1. What helps to explain why there are deserts on the west coasts of South America and southern Africa but not on the east coasts?

4 What happens to the amount of rain as you move away from the Equator to the tropic of Cancer? Include actual rainfall figures.

5 Why may winds blowing from over the land towards the sea be less likely to bring rain?

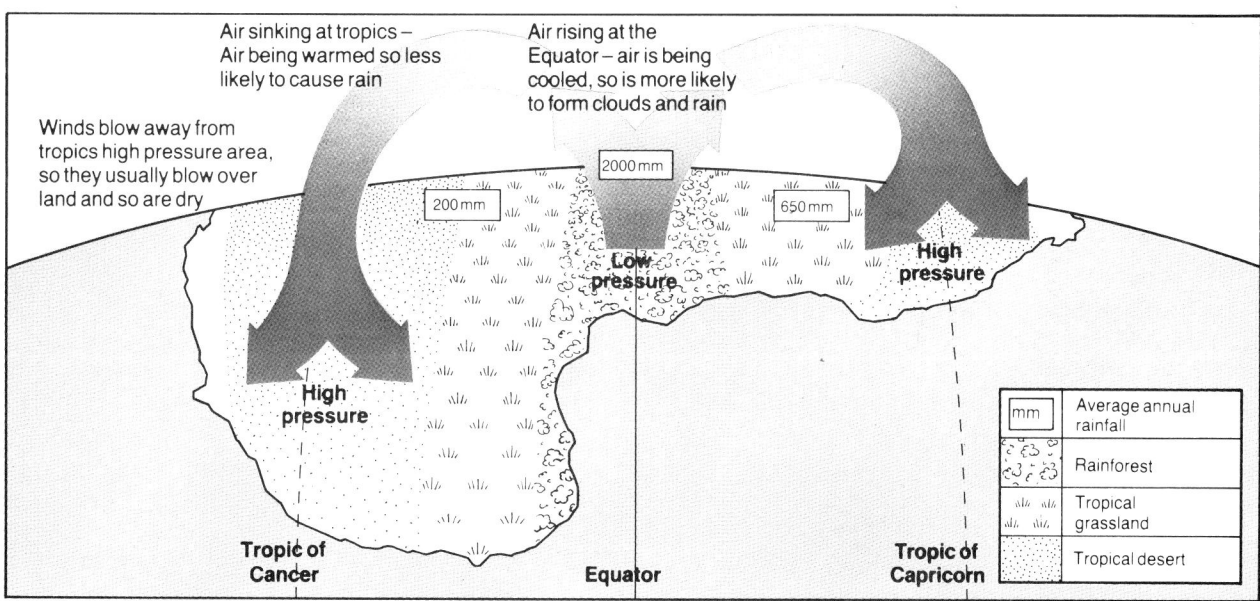

Figure 2: High and low pressure

Desert Environments

The Sahara is the world's largest desert. The British Isles would fit into it 26 times. Many people visualise the Sahara as being one vast area of sand. In fact only 10% is sand – the rest is stony or rocky, or made up of steep-sided ravines, hills and mountains. The sand 'seas' are perhaps the most dramatic areas as the desert wind builds the sand into huge curving ridges called **dunes**.

The landscapes of the world's deserts are very varied. What they have in common is a climate which is hot and dry. Daytime temperatures of 50°C in the shade are not unusual – in Britain the record temperature to date is 38°C! At night it can become cold and frosts may occur. This large daily **range of temperature** is due to the lack of clouds. They act rather like a blanket and help to reduce the loss of heat at night. In deserts, there are few clouds, so heat escapes rapidly. As it is cold, dew may form on the ground and it is this moisture that allows some plants and animals to survive in areas with little rainfall.

Desert areas receive less than 250 mm of rain a year – often it is much less. Ain Salah, in the Sahara, has an average rainfall of only 15 mm a year. Even this does not fall regularly and several years may pass with no rain at all. Then 30 mm may fall in a few hours on

Figure 1: Four desert landscapes (from top): Atacama Desert, Chile; Sahara Desert, Algeria; Monument Valley, Arizona, U.S.A.; Sahara Desert, Morocco

ground which is hard and dry. If the rainwater cannot soak into the earth, these sudden storms may result in **flash floods**. Experienced travellers never camp in dry watercourses as a rainstorm can rapidly turn a dry stream bed into a raging torrent.

After a fall of rain the desert can be transformed. Plant seeds that have been lying **dormant** quickly grow and flower and may produce a brightly coloured desert carpet.

The word 'desert' means uninhabited or uncultivated. This is not completely true in the world's hot deserts. If water is available then people can both live in and cultivate them. People have died from thirst when water has only been a few metres away. The water was of course below the ground. In some places this water reaches the surface and creates an **oasis**. Here, trees grow, people build their homes, crops are produced and animals graze (Fig. 2).

In Egypt, where 96% of the country is desert, 40 million people live either on the banks of the River Nile or around oases. The oases vary in size, the largest supporting several thousand people. Even in the Atacama, the driest area in the world, some agriculture takes place.

The Australian deserts generally receive more rain than the Sahara. The driest places usually have at least 125 mm of rain a year on average. Called the outback, it supports a number of

different deep-rooted trees and grasses which are adapted to the long periods of drought. These grasses may provide grazing for sheep. In the Thar or Great Indian Desert many of the wells are also religious shrines. It may be necessary to take off your shoes before approaching the well. Drawing water becomes a sacred ritual.

1 Why is there such a large daily range of temperature in deserts?

2 (a) Use Fig. 3 to draw two line graphs for Ain Salah. Draw a red line for the average maximum monthly temperatures and a blue line for the minimum.
(b) What is the biggest difference between maximum and minimum temperatures?

3 It is not only a lack of rain which can cause problems in the desert. What else is it about the rain which creates problems for people in the desert?

4 Why do you think the Indians living in the Thar Desert treat their wells like religious shrines?

5 Fig. 2 shows an oasis.
(a) Draw your own version of this and add the following labels: palm trees; mud-brick houses; fortress; surrounding desert.
(b) Explain why an oasis attracts people to live close by.

6 Four different types of desert landscapes are shown in Fig. 1. Match one of the following terms with each of the four different types of desert landscape: write a paragraph describing each photograph: sandy; stony; rocky hills; sun-baked earth.

Figure 3

Average Maximum and Minimum Temperatures for Ain Salah												
°C	J	F	M	A	M	J	J	A	S	O	N	D
Maximum	21	24	29	34	38	43	44	44	41	35	27	22
Minimum	7	9	11	16	20	27	28	28	26	19	11	8

How Animals and Plants Survive in the Desert

Deserts are not friendly places. To live in them, animals and plants have had to adapt. They have had to overcome the problems of little water, high daytime temperatures and cold nights. Animals also need to find food.

There is seldom much water to drink. Some animals can get all the liquid they need from their food or from body fat. Others drink vast quantities of water when it is available. Food is also often in short supply. It may be eaten and stored as fat in the body or collected and kept until needed.

Keeping cool is also essential. The body temperature must not rise much above normal or the animal will die. Many animals cool themselves by allowing water from their bodies to **evaporate**. Sweating and panting gets rid of unwanted heat but loses much precious water. Desert animals have to find other ways of keeping cool. Small animals hide underground where it is cooler during the day. Others go into a fitful sleep and let their body temperatures drop. By doing this the body 'burns' less food and both food and water are saved. This is called **aestivation**. Large animals such as the camel cannot burrow underground! They need other ways of staying cool without wasting water.

The camel (Fig. 2) can go for long periods without eating and drinking. Known as the 'ship of the desert' it has been used for

Figure 1: Saguaro cactus in the Arizona Desert, U.S.A.

many centuries to carry people and their goods. Camels are often bad tempered with smelly breath but are well adapted to survive in the desert.

When water is available the camel can drink up to 150 litres at one time. Green vegetation also provides some water. The camel's secret weapon is its hump. When food and water are plentiful it builds up fat in its hump. During shortages this hump gradually shrinks as the fat is 'burned-up' to produce energy. Water is also formed. The camel is able to allow its body temperature to fall

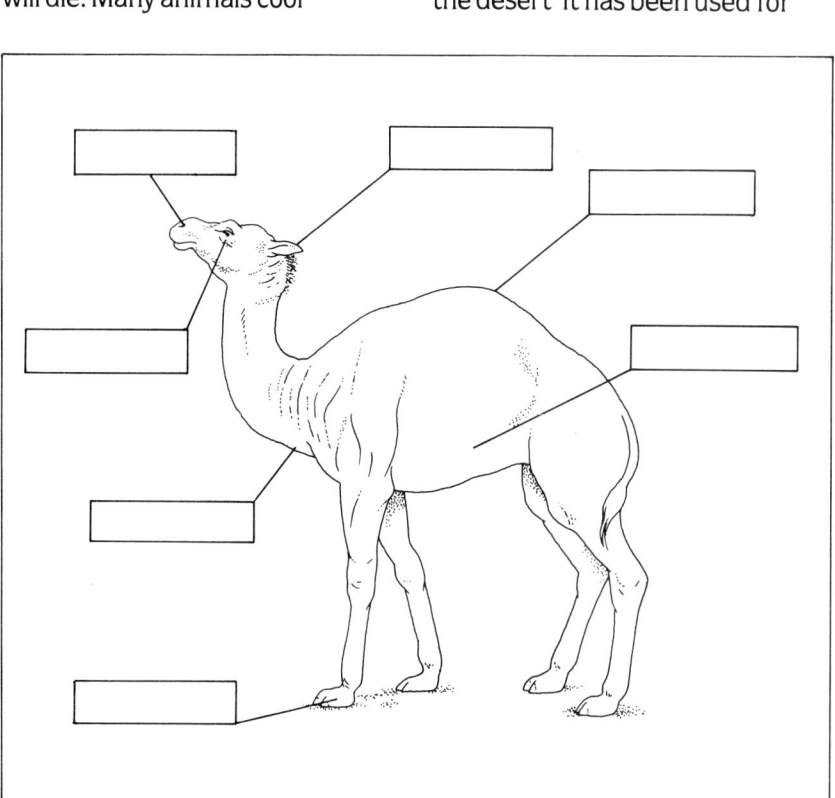

Figure 2: Camel

30

during the cold night. Normal body temperature is not regained until about mid-day. Only then does the camel need to use water to keep it cool. Its thick fur keeps it warm at night and helps to keep out the heat from the sun during the day.

Other adaptations include ear flaps, muscular nostrils, broad feet and long eye lashes. All these are helpful in the dusty, sandy desert conditions.

Many plants have also become adapted to the desert. Some have very short life cycles. They grow, bloom and produce seeds within a few weeks. The seeds lie on the dry ground until it rains and the process starts again. These are **drought evaders**. Plants like the Saguaro cactus (Fig. 1) are **drought resisters**. It stores water in its pulpy stem which slowly shrinks as it is used up. Long, shallow roots absorb any surface moisture which is quickly drawn up into the stem. The Saguaro also has thorns and not leaves. This saves water and provides protection. It can grow up to 15 m

high, and live for 200 years. Its pulpy stem, containing up to 90% water, can be 'mashed' to produce a drinkable liquid.

Trees such as the date palm grow long roots which can reach sources of underground water. Fig. 3 shows how useful this tree can be.

1 Copy Fig. 2 and then add the following labels to the correct boxes: *thick fur*; *fat store in hump*; *long eye-lashes*; *muscular nostrils*; *broad feet*; *ear flaps*; *body temperature varies*.

2 Explain in your own words why the camel is so well suited to life in the desert.

3 How do smaller animals cope with the problems of desert survival?

4 Briefly outline the three different ways in which plants may survive.

5 Copy Fig. 3 of the date palm and then say why it is such a useful tree.

Leaf or fronds used for mats, baskets and roofing

Young leaves eaten as vegetables or used as animal feed

Dates eaten fresh or dried. May be ground and used with millet flour

Trunk eventually used for timber

Palm wine made from sap or fermented dates

Tree gives shade

Crushed date stones used for animal feed

Long deep roots search for underground water

Figure 3: Date palm

6 With the help of Fig. 1 draw a picture of a Saguaro cactus. Add your own labels.

7 Fig. 4 shows a **camel caravan** crossing the desert. Why do you think the traders cross the desert in groups rather than by themselves?

8 **Project Idea:** Try to find out why the following animals are well suited to life in the desert: *spade-foot toad*; *jack rabbit*; *kangaroo rat*; *lizards*; *beetles*.

Figure 4: A camel caravan in Iraq

People in the Desert

People of the desert have to cope with hunger, thirst and sandstorms. Many have found special ways of surviving in desert lands. In the Negev Desert of southern Israel an ancient civilization lived as settled farmers with only 75-100 mm of rain a year. Their secret was to **terrace** the rocky hillsides and build canals to collect water from the nearby mountains. These were abandoned by AD 200 and since then the nomadic Bedouins have lived there. **Nomads** are people who move around with their livestock in search of fresh pasture.

Until 400 years ago the native Indian peoples of the Atacama Desert also used simple methods of irrigation. They understood how to live in harmony with the desert. The Spanish invaders brought goats and sheep which ate the delicate vegetation. They also cut down the trees for firewood and so made even more desert.

The Aborigines of the Australian deserts hunted animals and gathered fruits, berries and roots. The Europeans took their cattle and sheep to the desert fringes. In the early 1890s there were 13½ million sheep in western New South Wales. Then came terrible droughts. By the late 1890s there were only 3½ million sheep. The land has never recovered.

The nomadic tribes of the Sahara traded between the Mediterranean coast in the north and towns such as Timbuktu (Mali) and Kano (Nigeria) in the south. Camel caravans regularly crossed the desert. In addition to the hardships and dangers of everyday life they had to survive attacks by the Tuaregs. These desert warriors made their living by raiding caravans and capturing slaves.

The intense heat in the deserts has been overcome in different ways. The Bushmen of the Kalahari and the Aborigines (Fig. 3) wear little clothing. They avoid activity during the heat of the day. The search for food takes place in the cool of the early morning and at dusk. Their survival is based on their ability to understand and live closely with nature.

Most tribes in the Sahara and Arabian deserts cover themselves totally. Fig. 2 shows a Tuareg tribesman from the southern Sahara. Their dress keeps direct sun and wind from their bodies, keeps in the warmth at night and offers protection in sandstorms.

Figure 1: Tuareg camp in the Sahara Desert in southern Algeria

1 How do the traditional Bushmen and Aborigines survive in the desert lands where they live? You should include food supply and clothing in your explanation (see Fig. 3).

2 The nomads in the Sahara and Arabian deserts depend on very different methods of survival to the Bushmen and Aborigines. With the help of Fig. 1 describe their clothing and way of life.

3 Describe the nomads' home shown in Fig. 1. Why do they not build more permanent homes?

4 Nomads can only live in areas where there are few other people. Try to explain the reason for this.

5 How do you think the 'blue men' got their name? Fig. 2 should help.

6 How did the early peoples in the Negev Desert overcome the problem of very low rainfall?

Figure 2: Tuareg tribesman in distinctive blue clothing

7 Understanding nature is very important if people are to survive in the desert. With the help of the examples given, explain how people who do not understand the desert can make conditions even worse.

8 The following suggestions are intended to make travelling in the desert safer. For each one give reasons why it is important.
(i) Wear a hat
(ii) Wear sunglasses
(iii) Do not travel alone
(iv) Tell someone your route before setting out
(v) Take good, accurate maps
(vi) Learn how to trace faults and make simple repairs to your vehicle
(vii) Carry spare parts
(viii) Carry more food, fuel and water than you expect to use
(ix) Take a shovel and sand ladder
(x) Carry a tow rope
(xi) Stay with your vehicle if you break down

Figure 3: Aborigines in Northern Territory, Australia

Problems and Changes

Each year an area about the same size as Scotland turns into desert. Sometimes this is because the climate changes. More often it is due to the way people use the land. This making of new deserts is called **desertification**.

To the south of the Sahara Desert is a vast area of **semi-desert** known as the Sahel (Fig. 3). It is not as dry as the true desert and there is usually enough water and grazing for nomadic herders. Between 1968 and 1974 the Sahel experienced a severe drought. With very little rainfall the land was turned into desert. There was no longer enough pasture and water for the nomads and millions of animals and 250,000 people died. Many more people had to give up their nomadic way of life and move into the towns and cities. Most of them arrived with little or no money so they could not afford to buy houses. Their homes were tents or were made up from any materials available. These areas were called **shanty towns**. There would have been no sewers or running water, little food and few jobs. Two-thirds of Mauretania's population were nomads in 1968. By 1976 only one-third were still leading a nomadic life style.

Since 1974 there has been more rainfall in the Sahel, though it has varied in amount from year to year. However, some parts of the Sahel will remain as desert. This is not just because of lack of water, but because people and their animals have upset the delicate balance. Land that is **overgrazed** will not recover. For example, the

Figure 1: Goats eating thorn bushes in cleared woodland in the Upper Volta

Figure 2: A water hole in Senegal

nomads and their animals concentrated where new wells and water holes were built to help the drought-affected areas. The land around the water was heavily grazed – everything was eaten and the animals' hooves churned up the dry ground. This killed all the roots so that even when rain falls the vegetation will not grow again. As a result the area has been turned into true desert.

In some countries an increase in population can also lead to desertification. In the world's poorer countries there has been a welcome improvement in the standard of living for many of the people. This means that on average people are living longer and more infants are surviving the first few years of their lives. More people result in greater pressure on the land. In the poorer countries 90% of people use wood for heating and cooking. Trees are important for the land too – they protect the soil from wind and rain and their dead leaves put goodness back into the soil. More people mean that more wood is needed. Around a large town wood collecting can result in the cutting down of trees up to 100 km away. If too many trees are removed (Fig. 1) the land can gradually turn into desert.

More people also mean more pressure to grow food crops. Farmers plough up and plant crops on land that is really better suited to grazing animals. Once ploughed up it is more likely that the now unprotected, fertile top soil will be blown or washed away. In a few short years it can be turned into desert.

The discovery of oil has changed the life-style in some desert countries. Most of the new wealth is to be found in the cities and towns. In countries like Iran and Saudi Arabia this has attracted people away from the villages and country areas. It is often the young, healthy men who leave. This loss of labour means that the farmers who are left find it difficult to continue traditional farming methods. They concentrate on the land nearest to the village. This land is overused and the soil ruined. If the village is abandoned the ploughed fields rapidly become desert.

Desertification is not only happening in the poorer parts of the world. During this century overgrazing, widespread tree felling, and poor crop farming methods have turned millions of hectares of North America into desert and semi-desert. The United Nations estimates that it would take 40 years and £10,000 m just to reclaim the land throughout the world lost to desert in the last 25 years.

1 What do you understand by the word desertification?

2 Copy the map in Fig. 3 which shows the Sahel. Use an atlas to name the countries which make up the Sahel. The initial letters will help you.

3 Why has the drought in the Sahel forced many nomads to give up their way of life and move to the towns?

4 Fig. 1 shows one of the ways in which desertification can occur. How does collecting firewood help to make a desert and why are areas around towns and villages likely to lose most trees?

5 Too many animals may cause desertification. Explain the reasons for this. Why are areas around wells and water holes likely to suffer? (Fig. 2).

6 In many countries populations have grown very rapidly as standards of living have improved. How may this cause more land to become desert?

7 Imagine you are part of a nomadic family who have just arrived at a town. Describe what you think life would be like.

Figure 3: Countries of the Sahel

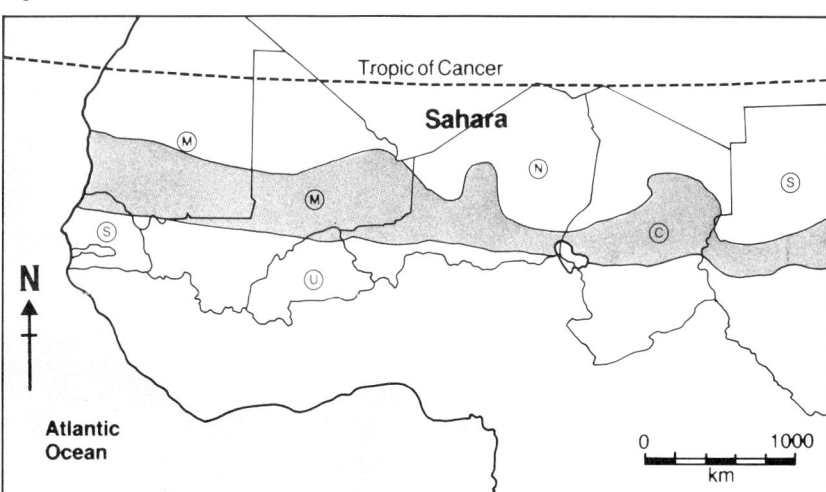

Water – Key to Development

Although it may not often rain in the desert it is sometimes possible to provide water by irrigating the land. With water, plants can grow and the desert can be turned green. Water may come from a river. For thousands of years the Egyptians have taken water from the River Nile. Traditional methods such as the shadouf (Fig. 2) are still used to raise small quantities of water to the higher land around the river. Canals carry greater amounts of water to areas such as Faiyum which is 100 km from Cairo. The water flows regularly all year thanks to the Aswan High Dam, completed in 1970. Pumps lift the water to 30 m above the canal to irrigate crops.

Other parts of Egypt use water from under the ground. Boreholes are drilled and the water pumped into irrigation canals. This water may contain a number of natural salts, such as sulphates, which tend to corrode the pipes and pumps.

Although irrigation means that areas with irregular or little rainfall can grow crops (Fig. 1) it has also created a number of serious problems. Without proper drainage an irrigated area may become waterlogged. Because it is so hot the water evaporates leaving a build-up of natural salts in the soil. Plants do not like salty soils. Drainage allows the salts to be washed through the top soil. Without good drainage much of the land at present being irrigated could finish up like the foreground in Fig. 1.

Figure 1: An irrigation network in Iraq

A regular supply of water has also meant that two or three crops a year may be grown in the same field. As a result more money has to be spent on fertilizers and pesticides. The high costs of modern irrigation mean that the land is often used to produce **cash crops**. The poor peasant farmer is unlikely to benefit from these schemes as he cannot afford the extra expense.

In Saudi Arabia, some irrigation water comes from the sea. It is necessary for the salt to be removed first in a process called desalination. This costs a lot of money. Selling their oil has provided the Saudis with the money to pay for their water.

In the Negev Desert the Israelis have spent vast sums of money. They have developed a system of trickle irrigation (Fig. 2). This involves thin plastic pipes with small holes which take precise amounts of water to each plant in a row of crops. In this way the roots receive the maximum quantity of water with the minimum of waste. As well as growing food for themselves, the Israelis produce roses, oranges, apricots, winter vegetables and other crops which are sold to Europe. Money from these cash crops pays for the expensive greenhouses and trickle irrigation pipes without which the area would remain as unproductive desert.

1 Describe the three sources of water that may be used for irrigation.

2 The Aswan High Dam is part of Egypt's irrigation programme.
(a) Use your atlas to draw a sketch map of the River Nile. Mark on Egypt, Sudan, the Mediterranean Sea, Cairo and the Aswan High Dam. Mark and name the new lake and the delta region.
(b) How do you think this lake helps Egypt to provide a regular supply of water for irrigation?
(c) The River Nile used to flood the land around the river, especially the delta region. Each year fertile silt carried by the river was left on the land after the floods. Now, the dam controls the flow of water and prevents the flooding. Explain how flood control has been both good and bad for the Nile valley.
(d) Hydroelectric power is also produced by the dam. As the dam is used for a number of different things it is said to be part of a multi-purpose water scheme. What are its three main purposes?

3 Many desert areas have water beneath the surface of the land. Why is this underground water often a problem for both the equipment and the plants?

4 Why is it so important to ensure that land being irrigated is also properly drained?

5 What is desalination? As there is plenty of sea water available why is it not used more for irrigation?

6 There are many ways of actually getting the water to the crops. Fig. 2 shows several methods.
(a) Which method do you think makes the best use of the water? Explain your decision.
(b) Money is a problem in many of the poorer countries which have deserts. Which method is most likely to be found in a poorer country? Give reasons for your answer.
(c) The Israelis have developed trickle irrigation. How does this work and why is less water wasted?

7 **Project Idea:** There are many irrigation schemes around the world. Try to find out more about one of them. Where does the water come from? How is it taken to the fields? What is grown? What did it cost, etc.

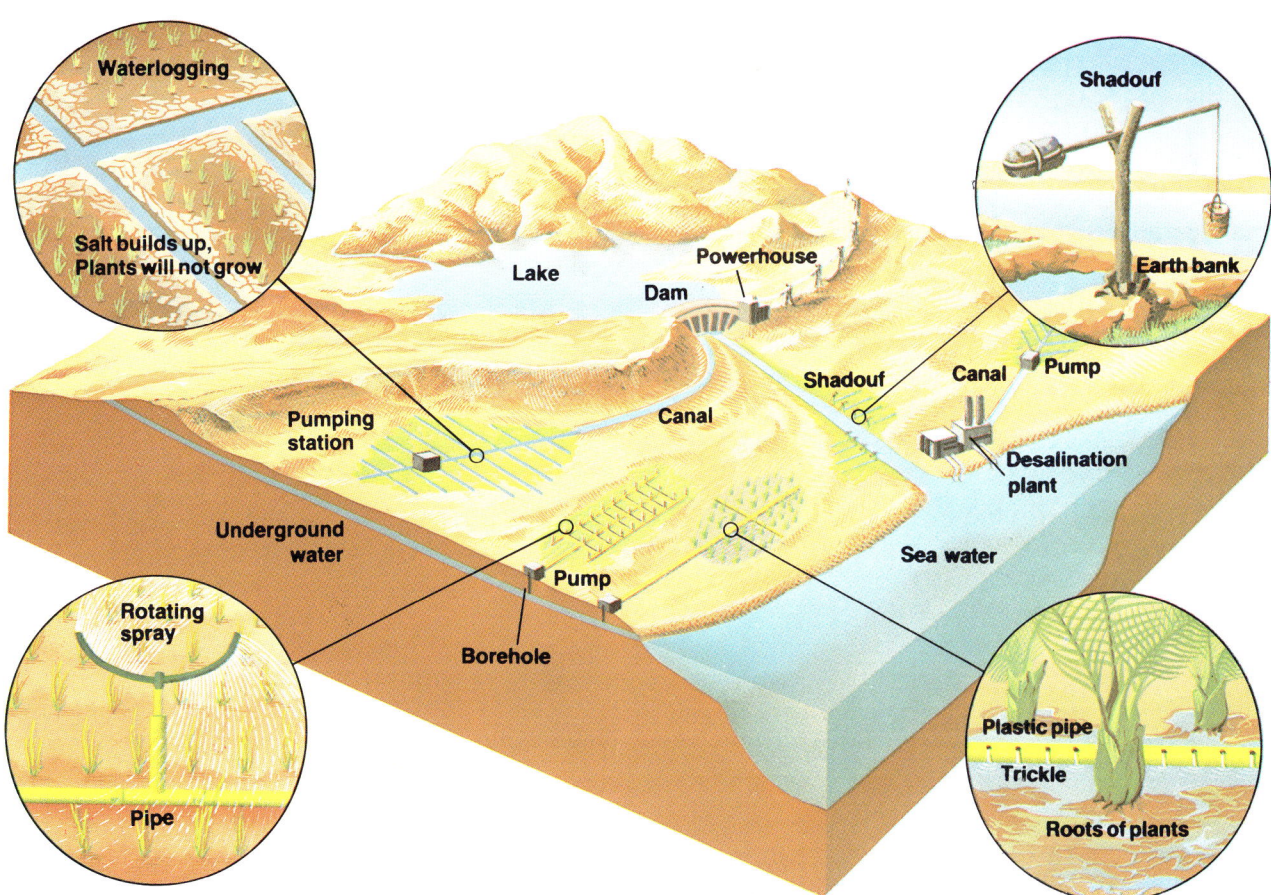

Figure 2: Irrigation in the desert

Using the River Satris – A Planning Game

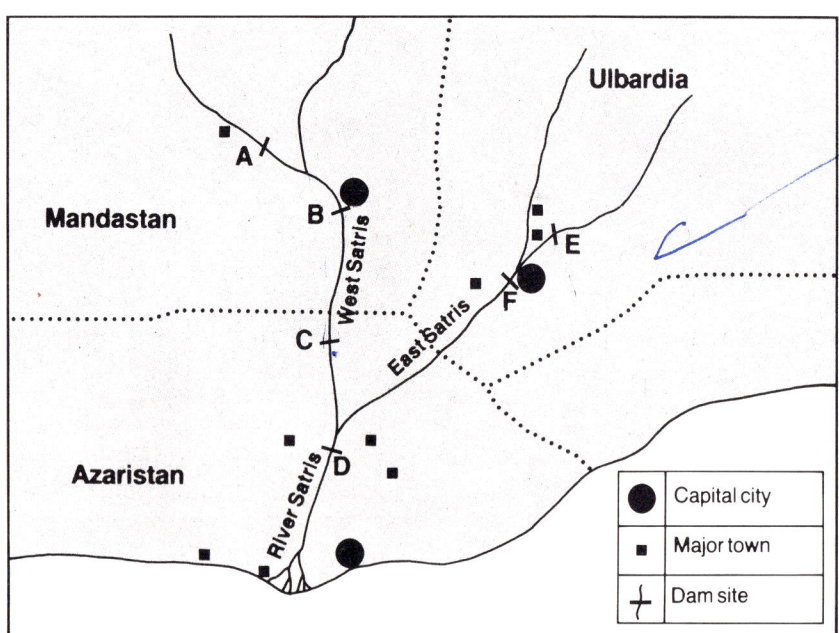

Figure 1: Using the River Satris

The River Satris is an imaginary river. As Fig. 1 shows, the Satris and its tributaries flow through three different countries. The water level in the rivers is high in the winter, but is very low in the summer. If the 'extra' winter river water could be held back by dams, it could be used to provide irrigation water during the summer. The dams could also be used to generate hydro-electric power. One problem though is that there is only a limited amount of water in the Satris – enough for another 1,000 units of irrigation water.

MANDASTAN

You are a very poor country. Most people are farmers. Enough food is grown for your own needs with some left to sell to Azaristan. Electricity would allow you to develop industries. An extra 400 units of water would produce another £20m worth of export crops each year.

Possible Schemes

Dam A Cost £200m
　　　Requires 300 units of water
　　　Provides 100 units of H.E.P.
Dam B Cost £400m
　　　Requires 400 units of water
　　　Provides 150 units of H.E.P.

You have £200m available. A £200m loan from the World Bank must be repaid after 10 years. Interest payable – £300m. Azaristan might offer a loan.

AZARISTAN

You are the wealthiest country but produce insufficient food for your people. Some is imported from Mandastan. You have several raw materials and export copper in its raw state. To develop your own copper industry a smelter would need a minimum of 200 units of H.E.P. increasing your copper exports by £80m a year.

Possible Schemes

Dam C Cost £500m
　　　Requires 600 units of water
　　　Provides 200 units of H.E.P.
Dam D Cost £1,000m
　　　Requires 500 units of water
　　　Provides 400 units of H.E.P.

You have £700m available. A £300m loan from the World Bank must be repaid after 10 years. Interest payable – £400m.

ULBARDIA

You are a poor country. Most of your people live in the river valleys and depend on farming. The river valleys are becoming overpopulated and you will need a minimum of 200 units of water to irrigate enough land to provide the extra food needed.

Possible Schemes

Dam E Cost £300m
　　　Requires 300 units of water
　　　Provides 100 units of H.E.P.
Dam F Cost £500m
　　　Requires 200 units of water
　　　Provides 200 units of H.E.P.

You have £300m available. An American company will give you an interest free loan of £200m to be repaid over 10 years. In return they want a cheap supply of electricity. They will pay £25m a year for 150 units of electricity.

Stage 1 – Deciding What to Do

Form into 4 groups. Each group represents one of the countries, or the United Nations Advisory Committee. Information about the countries and the committee is given in the boxes below. Read through your information box carefully, and then discuss what you should do. Which dam should you build? How would you pay for it?

Stage 2 – Sending Out Ambassadors – Information for the Countries

There is only a limited amount of water in the Satris. The other countries have a right to it as well, and there may not be enough water for all of the schemes.

UNITED NATIONS A.C.

Examine the available schemes and suggest what you think would be the best combination for the area as a whole. Remember that the river can provide only 1,000 units of irrigation water. Send advisors to each country to discuss your findings.

To help with the final decisions you must organise a summit meeting. Arrange for 3 experts from each country to meet and provide a chairperson to run the meeting. It is vital that agreement is reached.

Summary of Schemes

Dam	Cost	Water	H.E.P.
A	£ 200m	300 units	100 units
B	£ 400m	400 units	150 units
C	£ 500m	600 units	200 units
D	£1000m	500 units	400 units
E	£ 300m	300 units	100 units
F	£ 500m	200 units	200 units

Send one ambassador to each of the other countries. They must find out what other groups are planning to do. After they have reported back, discuss in your group what you should do now. Is there enough water for what all the countries want to do? Are you sticking with your original plan? Should you or the other countries change their plans?

Stage 3 – A Summit Meeting

Start the meeting by each team stating what it thinks would be the best scheme for its own country. The United Nations Advisory Committee then presents its plan.

There is only a limited amount of water so teams may need to negotiate with each other. If you cannot come to some agreement then none of you will be able to benefit properly. Is there a combination of schemes on which you can all agree?

Follow-up work

1 On a map mark on the details of the schemes that were finally agreed at the summit meeting.

2 Which scheme did you choose in the first place? Explain why you chose that scheme.

3 Did the discussions at the summit meeting result in any country changing its scheme? If so, why did they change?

4 Do you think that the final decision at the summit meeting was equally fair to all the countries, or did some countries do better than others? Explain your reasons as fully as you can.

5 Do you think that a summit meeting was a good way of deciding how to use the water of the Satris? How else could the countries have reached a decision?

The Akosombo Dam in Ghana, showing the turbine section

Rainforest – The Amazon

The Amazon is a world without winter. Plants can germinate, grow, flower and fruit at any time during the year. This is why it is always green. The plants make up the **equatorial rainforest**. As the first part of the name suggests, this type of forest is found near the Equator. This means it is always hot. The name also suggests that there is much rain. When it is hot and wet the air becomes very moist or humid. Wet clothes will not dry out unless they are exposed to direct sunlight. These are the sort of conditions you would expect to find in a hot-house. It is not surprising that plants grow well and quickly.

The Amazon rainforest covers an area between 6 and 7 million square kilometres, almost the size of Australia and 25 times that of the United Kingdom. It is home to about 1,800 species of bird, 2,000 species of fish, 15,000 species of insect and several hundred species of tree. The forest can be divided into a number of layers, see Fig. 2.

The tallest trees form the emergent layer. They receive the most sunlight. Below these giants are the medium-sized trees which form the upper canopy. These two layers are home to a number of small, light and active creatures. There are insects, brightly coloured birds, squirrel monkeys, the larger monkey-eating eagle, and many others.

The lower canopy blocks out most of the remaining sunlight from

This poisonous coral snake inhabits the Amazonian rainforest

the understory and forest floor. Each layer supports different animals and plants. The jaguar stalks the forest floor, the puma rests on a low branch, spider monkeys swing through the lower canopy. Piranha fish and alligators make swimming more exciting! The trees grow tall and straight. Most have shallow roots, some have buttresses at the base of their trunks and others stilt roots.

1 Fig. 1 shows the climatic information for Manaus in the centre of the Amazon rainforest.
(a) Draw rainfall and temperature graphs for Manaus.
(b) What is the annual temperature range (difference between the highest and lowest monthly temperatures)?
(c) What is the annual rainfall?
(d) Describe the climate of the Amazon rainforest.

2 Draw a simpler diagram of Fig. 2. Then mark on the main layers: emergent layer; upper canopy; lower canopy; understory; forest floor.

3 Paddling along the smaller rivers is like travelling through a huge tunnel lined by walls of trees. Try to explain why there is so little light at ground level.

4 **Project Idea:** Find out more about the animal life in the Amazon rainforest.
(a) Everyone in the class should select a different animal to draw and colour (eg. scarlet macaws, brilliantly coloured butterflies, strangely patterned frogs and toads, parrots, jaguars, alligators).
(b) Prepare a suitable frieze and stick your animals onto it in the right layers.

Figure 1

MANAUS	Average monthly temperature and rainfall											
	J	F	M	A	M	J	J	A	S	O	N	D
°C	28	27	27	27	27	27	28	28	28	29	29	28
mm	240	230	260	220	170	80	70	40	50	100	140	190

Figure 2

1 Monkey eating eagle
2 Squirrel monkeys
3 Toucan
4 Sloth
5 Howler monkeys
6 Macaw
7 Swallow-tail butterfly
8 Boa constrictor
9 Helicon butterfly
10 Tree frog
11 Peccary
12 Deer
13 Jaguar
14 Termite mound
15 Armadillo
16 Cayman
17 Poison-arrow frog
18 Lianas
19 Epiphytes
20 Buttress trunk
21 Stilt roots
22 Strangler fig
23 Palm
24 Skirt roots
25 Orchids

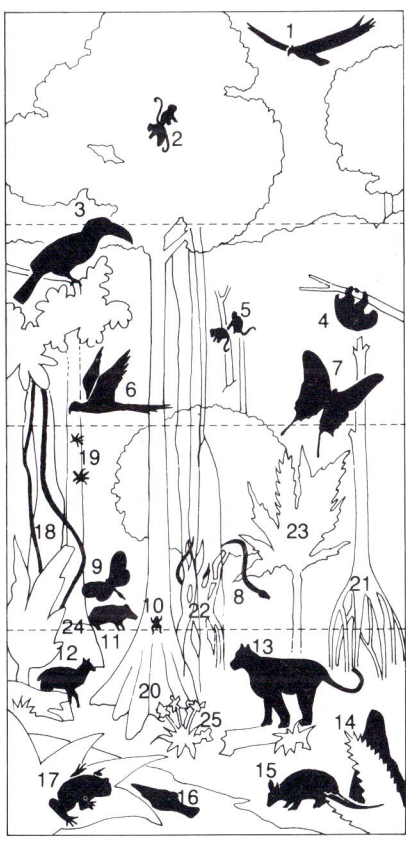

Emergent layer

Canopy
upper
lower

Understorey

Water/forest floor

People of the Amazon Rainforest

The Amazon rainforest has been called a human desert. Although the vegetation looks rich and green it is not easy for people to find food. As a result, the Amazon Indians live in small groups scattered throughout the vast area. Most of them live close to a river in self-contained villages and have little contact with their neighbours. They live in communal houses called malocas. Three or four families share each maloca. Fig. 1 shows the men of a village building a maloca.

Hunting and fishing provide some food but most Indian groups depend on farming. In general Amazon soils are poor and in order to produce enough food the Indians must move from place to place. A patch of forest is cleared and the felled trees and undergrowth burned. The ash adds goodness to the soil and helps to produce crops for a year or two. When the fertility is exhausted they abandon the plot and move on. A fresh area is

Figure 1: Building a maloca

cleared, the trees and undergrowth burned and so on. This type of **shifting cultivation** is known as slash-and-burn. The main crop is manioc, a type of cassava, which with fish provides the basis of most meals. Maize, cotton, tobacco and other crops are also grown. Small groups moving around such a huge area do little damage to the rainforest. Unfortunately a growing population caused by people moving into the rainforests from other areas has put pressure on what is really a delicately balanced environment.

The luxuriant vegetation in the Amazon rainforest is misleading. The soils are in fact not rich. They are poor and contain few nutrients. Forest plants are able to grow so well because the forest acts rather like a huge sponge. Nutrients are absorbed from the rain and the atmosphere. When dead leaves and wood fall to the ground they decompose and their nutrients are taken up by the **root mat**. This is made up of humus, fungi and other micro-organisms. It may be up to 30 cm thick. It is called a mat because it is separate from the soil below. In experiments over 99% of available nutrients have been absorbed by the root mat and so re-cycled to the living trees. Few nutrients reach the soil underneath. When the forest is cleared and the root mat destroyed little fertility is left in the soil. Crops rapidly exhaust what little goodness there is and yields decrease. Close to the main rivers annual flooding does keep the soils more fertile.

Amazonian Indians taking home an anaconda which they have killed

Figure 2: Slash-and-burn agriculture

1 Why do you think that many villages are built close to rivers?

2 Fig. 1 shows a maloca being constructed.
(a) What materials are being used to build it?
(b) Where do these materials come from?
(c) What do you think happens to these houses when the families move on?

3 In Fig. 2 you can see a typical cleared plot in the rainforest.
(a) Draw your own version of this picture.
(b) Add the following labels to your picture: thick tree stumps left; surrounding dense forest; burnt tree trunks provide shade for young plants; manioc planted in earth mounds; simple tools used for cultivation.

4 In your own words explain how the slash-and-burn method of farming operates. Why is this type of agriculture used in the Amazon rainforest?

5 In the past it was often a hundred years or more before the same area of land was cleared again for cultivation. With the recent increase in the number of people farming in the Amazon rainforest there is more pressure on the accessible land. What effect may this have?

6 Dead leaves and fallen trees decompose very quickly in the rainforest. What happens to the nutrients produced when they are broken down?

7 The rainforest is made up of large, healthy, fast-growing plants. When the Amazon rainforest is cleared farmers can only produce poor crops for a year or two. Try to explain the reason for this.

8 Draw a diagram to show the relationship between a living tree, decaying material, the root mat and the soil.

9 **Project Idea:** Using twigs, leaves and other suitable materials make a model of an Indian village. Include Molocas, a cleared plot and the surrounding rainforest.

Exploration and Development in the Amazon

The Amazon is a mighty river. In 24 hours it empties as much water into the Atlantic Ocean as the River Thames carries past London in a year! Until fairly recently the river was the only way to gain access to the interior of the rainforest. The first European discovery of the Amazon was in 1499. It was not until 1542 that a Spanish captain crossed the Andes in Ecuador and sailed down the River Napo (Fig. 3) into the Amazon and on to the Atlantic. During the eighteenth and nineteenth centuries many explorer-scientists were attracted by the wealth of plants and animals which could be found in the Amazon rainforest.

Wild rubber brought prosperity for a short while to the area around Manaus (Fig. 3). From 1890-1912 there was a rubber boom following the invention of the pneumatic tyre. Manaus built an opera house (Fig. 1), a palace of justice, a telephone network, a tram system and a floating harbour. Ships sailed regularly to Liverpool in England. Competition from the new rubber plantations in South-East Asia brought the

Figure 1: The opera house in Manaus

boom to an end. For nearly 50 years the region remained unimportant and untouched. Poor communications, hostile Indians, the discomfort of stings and diseases, vast distances, dense rainforest and a general fear of the unknown made it an uninviting place.

Then in 1960 the new capital at Brasilia was officially opened. This signalled a greater interest in the north and west of Brazil. New roads were built linking the capital to Belem and Porto Velho on the edge of the rainforest (Fig. 3).

Most of Amazonia still had a poor population living in isolated settlements linked only by irregular boat services and a limited and expensive air service. Boats were very slow. From Rio Branco downstream to Manaus took anything from 12 to 18 days!

In 1970 the Brazilian government announced a massive road building programme. This would give access to new farm land and create opportunities for

Figure 2: A highway being built through the Amazon

lumbering, mining and cattle ranching. Some large companies from outside Brazil have invested in the area as a result. Another reason for this sudden interest was due to a series of droughts in North-East Brazil. Men from the drought affected region could be employed on road-building projects. North-easterners would be able to obtain 100 hectare plots alongside the new 'highways'. It was proposed that 100,000 families would move into Amazonia between 1972 and 1977. They would live in new settlements constructed 5 to 10 km apart. There would be homes for 50 families, a primary school and health post.

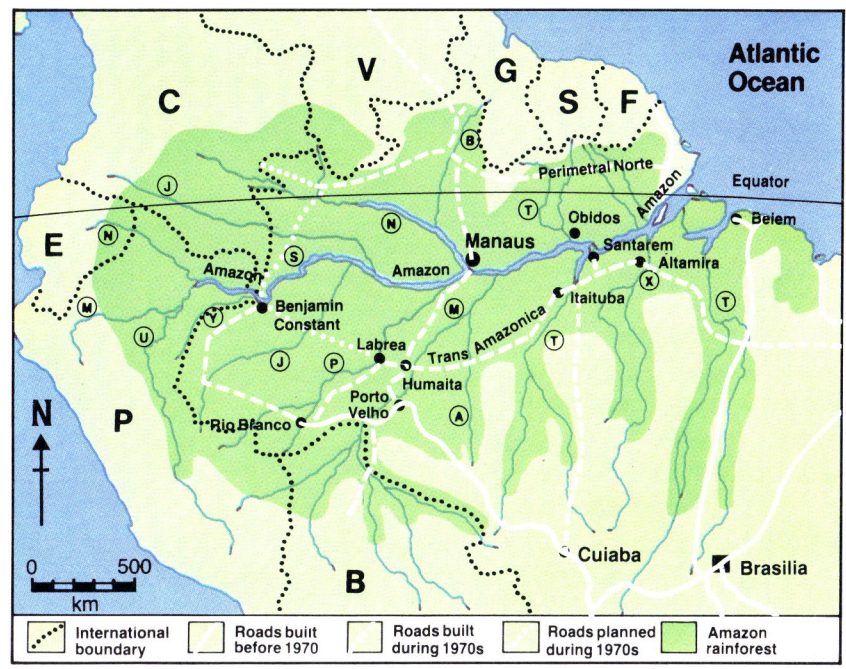

Figure 3: Amazonia

The major new road was the Trans Amazonica Highway (Fig. 2). By 1974 it had reached Humaita (Fig. 3) and by 1976 linked Labrea. Other roads run from north to south. Cuibá to Santarem built by the army and finished in 1976, and Porto Velho to Manaus, opened in 1972. In the north another new road, the 'Perimetral Norte' will eventually complete the network (Fig. 3).

1 Fig. 3 is a map of the northern part of South America.
(a) Draw your own map to include the coastline, the rivers, the rainforest and the international boundaries.
(b) Use your atlas to name the eight countries represented by the letters B, C, E, F, G, P, S and V.
(c) Sixteen of the larger rivers have been marked with the first letter of their names. Use your atlas to find their names and put them in a key.
(d) Most of the rivers rise in one of three highland areas. Use your atlas to mark on the Guiana Highlands, the Mato Grosso and the Andes.
(e) Why have the rivers always been an important method of communication?
(f) Work out the distance between Rio Branco and Manaus. If the journey takes an average of 15 days, at what speed would you be travelling? Would it be faster or slower on the return journey? Explain why.

2 In your own words explain why the Amazon region was uninviting.

3 Wild rubber trees are scattered over a wide area in the rainforest. On a plantation they are grown close together. Try to suggest why rubber from South-East Asia was more successful than that from Brazil.

4 The building of roads into Amazonia has been a recent development.
(a) On your map mark on the roads which were built by 1970.
(b) Briefly explain where these roads are found in relationship to the rainforest.
(c) Now mark on the roads built and planned during the 1970s.
(d) About half of Brazil is made up of rainforest. It is the sort of area in which it is difficult to enforce national boundaries. Brazil shares boundaries with seven of her neighbours in or around the rainforest. Do the roads help Brazil with her national security? Explain your answer.
(e) What else may the roads help to develop in Amazonia?

5 In what way did a drought in North-East Brazil affect Amazonia?

6 **Project Idea:** Many important scientific expeditions have been to the Amazon. See if you can find out more about leaders of these expeditions, such as Francisco de Orellana, La Condamine, Humboldt, Wallace, Bates, Spruce and Fawcett, or any one else you know about.

Problems of Development

'From green hell to red desert.' That is one view of the present changes in Amazonia. It is estimated that 100,000 square km of rainforest were destroyed in Brazil during 1975. Much of this was due to the better access provided by the new roads. At the same time many more people arrived in the region to farm, mine or work in the growing towns. The town of Altamira grew from 2,800 in 1970 to 18,500 by 1976. This development has put increasing pressure on the rainforest – the plants, animals and Indians.

Figure 1: Clearing the rainforest near Manaus

Much of the cleared land is productive for only two or three years without fertilizer. It is cheaper to abandon it and clear more of the forest. Without the dense covering of trees the heavy tropical downpours wash away the exposed top soil. Without the tree roots to absorb water there is also greater danger of flooding.

The new roads cost a lot to build (Fig. 1). Few of them have asphalt surfaces. In the dry season the dirt roads become very dusty. They often flood and become impassable when it is very wet. They are also expensive to maintain and heavy lorries damage them. Bolivia and Venezuela are the only countries with international road links. If the Trans Amazonica continued across Peru it would provide an important link with the Pacific Ocean. Higher petrol prices have made the Brazilian government think more seriously about improving water transport.

Some of the new roads have interfered with the traditional way of life of the Indians. In places the roads have split tribal groups. Many Indians have died from 'common' illnesses brought into Amazonia by the new arrivals. Colds, measles and 'flu have all been killers. A general lack of understanding about the amount of land needed to support small numbers of Indians has resulted in their territories being used for cattle ranching and for farming by the new settlers. Other Indian groups have been moved into **reserves** which have been set up by the Brazilian government. This usually means poorer soils and a limited area in which to hunt and cultivate the land.

There are many fears about the result of destroying the rainforests. Some scientists believe that world temperatures may rise. This could cause problems for farmers in other parts of the world. It could also make ice melt at the poles. Other scientists think that the trees are an important reason for the high rainfall in Amazonia. Without them rainfall might be much less and the area could become a desert. It is not certain what would actually happen.

The rainforests are important for all of us. They provide coffee, cocoa, bananas, rubber, Brazil nuts, and many other useful products. The medical and scientific worlds are still finding important natural substances. It is hoped that in the future the tropical rainforests will provide vital cures for diseases such as cancer.

The desire to extract wealth as quickly as possible is a real threat. New machines can clear a hectare of rainforest in two hours. Should a forest which has taken thousands of years to develop be turned into cardboard and brown paper?

1 Look at Fig. 2 on page 44 and Fig. 1 and then try to explain what you think is meant by 'from green hell to red desert'.

2 The 100,000 square km of rainforest cleared in 1975 represented about 4% of the forest remaining in Brazil.
(a) If the same rate of destruction continued, how long would it be before the rest of the rainforest disappeared?
(b) Do you think all of the rainforest will be cut down? Give reasons for your answer.
(c) What do some scientists think might happen if all of the rainforest was removed?
(d) If the ice at the poles did melt, how might this effect the rest of the world?

3 Building roads through the rainforest was not easy.

(a) Why is driving on these roads often difficult or unpleasant?
(b) The Trans Amazonica cost about $55,000 a kilometre to build. Use Fig. 3 on page 45 to work out the approximate cost of the road between Altamira and Labrea.
(c) Do you think it was worth spending so much money on a road which does not really go anywhere? Explain your answer.
(d) If Peru was prepared to build a road to join up with the Trans Amazonica how would this help Brazil?
(e) What effects have higher petrol prices had on road transport?

4 The Amazon Indians had little contact with 'outsiders' in many parts of the rainforest until the new roads were built.
(a) Why have many Indians died

since making contact with outsiders?
(b) What is surprising about this?
(c) Many Indian children now have the chance to go to school. Indian families can receive medical attention (Fig. 2). Do you think this makes up for the loss of their traditional way of life?

5 Write an account explaining what you consider to be the good and bad effects of developing the rainforest.

6 **Project Idea:** People use many of the natural products from the rainforest. Illustrate some of these with drawings, labels or the actual product. Try to find out how quinine and curare are used. Are there any other plants used for medical or scientific purposes which you think you can add to this list?

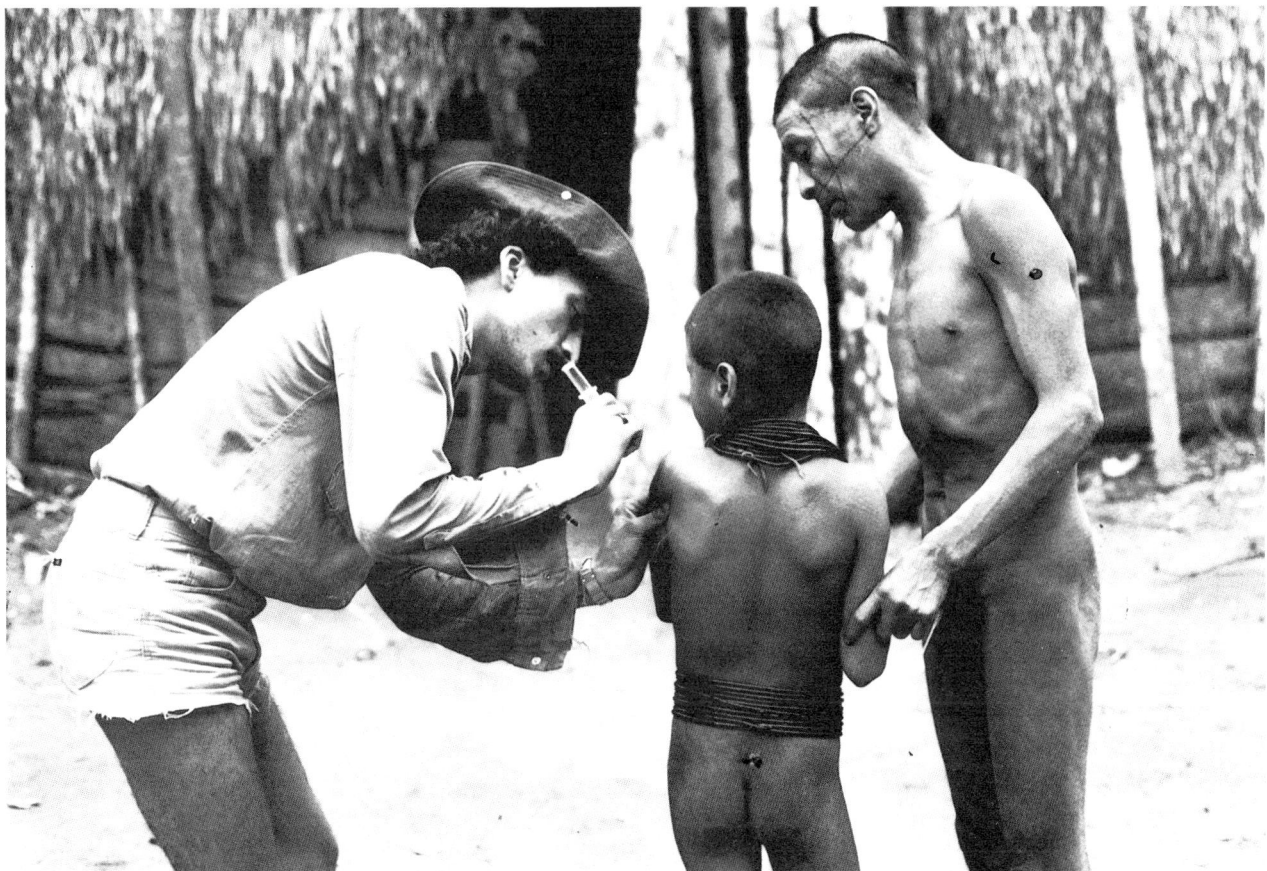

Figure 2: A doctor inoculating a reservation Indian against smallpox

Glossary

Active Layer: The soil above the **permafrost** which thaws during the summer months.

Aestivation: A process by which some animals can allow their body temperatures to drop while **dormant** during the summer months. This helps to save food and water.

Alp: An area of mountain pasture.

Camel caravan: A group of people and their camels travelling together across hot deserts. They are often used to transport goods for trade.

Cash crops: Crops grown so that they can be sold to make money rather than to be eaten by the farmers and their families.

Corrie: A deep, rounded basin with steep sides formed by the action of snow and ice. It may also be called a cirque or cwm.

Desertification: The process of turning marginal land into unproductive desert. This is often due to mismanagement of the land.

Deserts: Areas where there is generally very little rain each year, where few plants can grow, and few animals live. There are hot and cold deserts.

Dormant: A state of inactivity as during sleep.

Drought: A prolonged period of dry weather often resulting in the failure of crops.

Drought evaders: Plants which overcome a long period of dry weather by producing seeds which lie **dormant** until it rains.

Drought resisters: Plants which survive during long periods of dry weather by storing moisture when it is available.

Dunes: Hills or ridges of sand built up by the wind.

Environmentalists: People who specialise in trying to protect the land and wildlife from unsuitable development.

Equatorial rainforests: Hot, wet evergreen forests growing close to the Equator; sometimes called jungles. They are made up of a number of different layers of vegetation.

Erosion: The wearing away of the land surface by ice, water or wind.

Evaporate: To change from a liquid or solid state to a vapour.

Flash flood: A sudden flood caused by torrential rainfall when the water cannot soak away because the ground is too hard or dry. They often occur in deserts.

Glacier: A mass of ice which moves slowly down a valley and erodes it into a U-shape.

Herbivorous: Eating plants – including berries, grass and roots – but not meat.

Hibernate: To remain inactive or **dormant** during the winter months.

Ice-cap: A vast and often very deep mass of snow and ice covering the land. It forms a cold desert where few plants and animals can survive.

Midnight sun: When in midsummer the sun does not sink below the horizon during a 24 hour period within the Arctic and Antarctic circles. Therefore it can be seen at midnight.

Natural resources: Anything which occurs naturally, and which people find useful, such as minerals, water or oil.

Nomads: People who move around with their livestock in search of fresh pasture or food.

Oasis: An area in the desert made fertile by the presence of water at or close to the surface.

Overgrazed: The destruction of vegetation due to too many animals using a restricted area of land. This often happens around a well or waterhole.

Permafrost: Ground that is always frozen.

Permanent snow line: The line above which snow never melts, even in the summer.

Range of temperature: The difference between the highest and lowest temperature during a given time.

Reserves: Areas of land set aside for people to live in when their original lands are taken over by other people and used for other purposes.

Root mat: In Equatorial rainforests this is the top layer of soil where most of the goodness and plant roots are found. It is easily destroyed when trees are cleared.

Semi desert: An area on the fringes of the true desert. More plants and animals can survive here than in the desert.

Shanty town: A section of a town or city where very poor people live. Their homes are assembled from any available materials and usually lack basic services such as running water and sewers.

Shifting cultivation: A method of simple farming involving the clearing of an area of land which is then only used for a short time until it becomes infertile. Another area is then cleared.

Terraces: Artificial steps of flat land which allow cultivation of steep hillsides.

Tundra: Cold, treeless plains found in northern Europe, North America and Asia. Mosses, lichens and some flowering plants grow during the short summers.

U-shaped valley: A mountain valley carved or eroded by a glacier.